CONTENTS

Introduction – 3
The House Theory – 4
John Doe Diaries Part I – 6
The Attitudes of Fear – 7
The Dawn of Individuality – 13
- Beginning to question – 13
- Absorbing Everything – 15
- The Shadow of Doubt – 21
The Embracing of Facade – 25
- A Moment to Pause – 25
- The Facade – 29
- Refusal to Challenge – 31
- Effects of losing Individuality – 32
How We Embrace Stagnation – 40
- Seeing the results – 40
- Resistance to Change – 43
- Support Groups – 55
John Doe Diaries Part II – 61
Perceived "Positives" of the 'House' – 62
- Safety – 64
- Avoidance of Terror – 66
- Better Relationships – 68
- Being Loved – 71
- Less Responsibility – 72
- Togetherness – 73
- Less Threats – 73
How the 'House' Affects Others – 76
- Exclusivity – 77
- Verbal Abuse – 81
- Physical Abuse – 84
- War – 88
The 'House' Emotions – 94

    - Fear of Being Wrong – 95
    - Terror of Authority – 105
How the 'House' Affects us Personally – 110
    - Lack of Emotional Responsibility – 117
    - Grief of Truth – 125
John Doe Diaries Part III – 130
The Solution – 131
    - Humility – 132
    - Vision – 138
    - Desire – 142
    - Bravery – 148
My Final Message – 154
    - My Experience – 154
John Doe Diaries Part IV – 157
Bibliography – 160

THERE IS NO GREY AREA:
A Moment of Pause

The Introduction

It's within you! I can see, feel, and believe it. I believe it so much that I am willing to go against everything I once knew in order to see you happy, never sell yourself short.

The 1999 classic film The Matrix, was about a guy who initially believed in the world around him, only to realise he was in a dreamworld. During a scene in the film, the main character Neo sees a boy bending a spoon with what looks like his mind. The boy then begins to explain the truth to Neo. The truth was that using force to bend the spoon was impossible, instead he had to realise there is no spoon; it was only himself that was bending.

It takes a single moment of pause to contemplate a different reality, to grasp something that we missed. Our entire future has the potential to curve and improve within those fleeting moments.

According to the Cambridge Dictionary, the term 'grey area' means "a situation that is not clear, or where the rules are not known".

So what do I mean by "there is no grey area"?

You can think of it as a state of mind but what I really mean is simple. Outside of art, I believe there is an absolute truth to everything and that constantly questioning one's self and the surrounding environment will eventually unlock that truth. Luckily, we are born with an innate quality of curiosity. It is unfortunate then that typically out of fear, and as we get older we eventually stop asking obvious and basic questions. Questioning our own reality can and will be scary, but it is the truth that will set us free. It is only then that we realise there is no spoon.

The 'House' Theory

Due to my own desire to question things around me, I couldn't help but notice the same pattern happening again and again and in so many different ways. So I came up with the House Theory to be able to easily explain myself. At the time, I had no intention of putting it in a book, but when I sat down and thought about the topic of my book, I knew that the House Theory would be a great point to base my book around.

The house theory is this: Imagine you have a house, and in this house there are as many people as you can think of; the number of people doesn't matter. Now, inside this house, every single one of those people has the same beliefs or feelings. The problem with this house is not the belief itself; it is the people who choose to hold onto the belief. We hold onto beliefs for many reasons, but you can see that if those people in the house refuse to question their beliefs, why it would then be hard for them to change, and instead of taking maybe a couple of hours to change through simple questioning, it takes generations and effects generations of people.

Now, if you expand that idea into a multitude of different scenarios, you can see that in many ways humankind has been halted drastically, and even though, yes, we have changed a lot even in the last 100 years in loving ways, such as allowing women to vote, more acceptance of people's sexualities and cultures. However, imagine what we could accomplish if we began to embrace questioning from the very beginning. Unfortunately, we are terrified of leaving our house, we are terrified of disagreeing with our social groups, society, or even our own families. Many times in the past, we have been ridiculed for doing so, we have been mocked, and we have been threatened and sometimes beaten. The best part about the house, for all its flaws, is that it can take a single brave individual to look through its holes and see the truth. Embracing their individuality and their right to question the surrounding reality could cause other people to do the same and inevitably bring the 'house' down.

John Doe Diaries Part I

Walking along this neighbourhood I see several houses; a number of them are as big as Buckingham Palace, and a few are as small as a garden shed. If I listen closely, I can hear them talking, plotting their next move, and I can see the shadow of the individual in their shed at night. No, I do not know these people, but we share common ground; we all feel the need to be protected, and so we inhabit these houses. Some of these houses go way back to the first century; while they might look old and withered, they have stood the test of time, and that is the other purpose of every single house, to survive. It doesn't matter what bumps and bruises each of us gets along the way as long as we stick to our conviction. It isn't about the individual; it's about the team, and so from the moment we enter through the door we trade our garments for the team uniform. It's a tradition that goes back to when the first house was built, sort of like wearing costumes on Halloween, except this is permanent; no, no, we can never take them off. The last person I saw take theirs off, well... let's just say things didn't end well.

So here I am walking the streets of this neighbourhood, finding places to call home like so many others before me. Houses with a familiar voice seem to attract most, and this time I hear that voice. I see one of the houses I belong to, and as I jog up those steps, a familiar person greets me, although I cannot see their face clearly I can feel we have some sort of history. As I walk into the house, the doors shuts behind me, darkness sets in, and there are no lights. The only light that we can see is coming from a hole in the wall, but I do not fret; after all we are all one.

The Attitudes of Fear

Humanity has presumably experienced fear to some extent, going all the way back to the dawn of man. Many different philosophers have felt differently about fear. Lucius Annaeus Seneca the Younger, who was a stoic philosopher in ancient Rome who was usually just known as Seneca, said, *"limiting one's desires actually helps to cure one of fear. Cease to hope and you will cease to fear"*. On the other hand, you have Aristotle who said, *"He who has overcome his fears will truly be free."* There are many different ways you can look at fear, for some fear has been comforting, that voice inside you that tells you whether or not you can trust a person, whether you should run away or hide, and in many cases our fear may have saved our lives. For others, fear is a hindrance, like a straitjacket that we just can't seem to shake; we cannot seem to find the key that would enable us to do the very things we wish to do at any given moment, I can personally relate to that one more. For many, we wish to avoid fear like the plague, in some cases take any action possible, regardless of its consequences to avoid the very thing we're afraid of coming true.

There are many more examples of how we feel about fear, and it is possible that we may have experienced all these feelings at some point in our lives. Regardless of how we feel, fear still remains, and regardless of how much we take action to avoid it, it still rears its ugly head. I feel there is a general feeling that fear is either a necessity for mankind to exist or that it is not worth worrying about because we cannot do anything about it. The issue is, do we really understand the extent of our fear? Do we truly see the full consequences of holding onto such an emotion? Are the benefits of fear valid, or are they overemphasised?

There are many different types of fears, many of which we may feel serve as valid reasons for existing. Now, I am not going to go through all of them because I'm sure you can guess what some of them are; however, one of them that caught my attention was cynophobia which is an intense fear of dogs. When I was about 12 years old, I would take a certain route to school every day, and on that route would be a dog, completely loose with no owner or leash in sight; At that time, I had an intense fear of dogs, which I still have to this day, but it has lessened since then. The dog wouldn't be there all the time; it would be there roughly 2 days out of the 5 days I would walk to school. Most days I would weave in and around the cars to stay out of its sight, some days I would take a different route when I knew he was there. However, on one particular day, I saw the dog at the last minute, and he chased me down. I was in so much fear that I ran into the road trying to get away from it, and a car was practically inches from running me over.

My fear almost drove me to be physically harmed. I do understand that it is possible that my fear also potentially saved me from being harmed on other occasions. But what was the possible truth of the moment? It is possible that the dog did not wish to bite me at all but instead didn't want me to be around him. It is also possible that due to my fear, I made certain movements or had a specific body posture that told him I was anxious or nervous, and so the dog pounced. Whatever the reason, it is possible that if I desired to understand the dog and understood how to read them, that none of this would have happened, and I would have little reason to be afraid. Many children do not grow up afraid of dogs; some see them as their favourite animal, and anytime they see a dog, they become excited and inquisitive. So then the question becomes, why me? Why are so many not just afraid of dogs but also afraid of spiders, snakes, and so on. Some of us, like myself, have never been bitten by a dog, a snake, or a spider before and yet we are frightened of it.

Healthline.com did an article on "Zoophobia: The Fear of Animals," which was created by Jill Seladi-Schulman on January 11th 2021, and was medically reviewed by Timothy J. Legg. Schulman states in the topic of 'What causes a fear of animals', *"Having a negative experience with an animal may cause you to fear it."* She also states, *"We may also learn to fear animals from someone who is close to us, such as a parent or sibling. For example, if your parent is terrified of spiders, you may learn to fear them as well."* She also states as a cause, *"There's a possibility that genetics may also play a role in specific phobias."* You can understand why someone who experiences something bad would become afraid of it so that they avoid encountering that same experience, but we do not avoid it. It might limit how much we encounter the fear, but we do not avoid it completely. All it does is limit our experience and confine our ability to express ourselves. Now, if there was a possibility that we could genetically pass it down to our children or teach other people to be afraid, surely that would be cause for concern. Surely we wouldn't want our children or the people we teach to limit their personalities or how much freedom they have.

Is it our fear that gives us our ability to react quickly to danger? Is our fear so tied tightly to our survival that we cannot take a basic action, such as ducking without it? NorthWesternMedicine.org wrote an article on October 2020 that stated, *"Fear is experienced in your mind, but it triggers a strong physical reaction in your body. As soon as you recognise fear, your amygdala (small organ in the middle of your brain) goes to work. It alerts your nervous system, which sets your body's fear response into motion. Stress hormones like cortisol and adrenaline are released. Your blood pressure and heart rate increase. You start breathing faster. Even your blood flow changes – blood actually flows away from your heart and into your limbs, making it easier for you to start throwing punches, or run for your life. Your body is preparing for fight-or-flight."* It is fair to say that fear or stress causes the fight or flight response; it is automatic. However, as I demonstrated with my personal example about the dog, my flight response almost got me seriously injured. I understand there is a counterargument to that, but it is interesting that even though in the moment we may be fighting or flighting to get away from potential trauma or injuries that we encounter them anyway, is it not possible to argue that without such automatic decisions we might be completely fine? I mean, its hard to imagine at this moment in time, but to me, it's worth finding out.

Is fear a natural emotion? First, the word natural must be defined. According to the Cambridge Dictionary, the word natural means *"as found in nature and not involving anything made or done by people"*. So it has to be found in nature to be considered natural, which makes sense, but to me, that does pose a question, do animals feel fear? Cassie Freund at Wake Forest University wrote an article on October 31st, 2017 on a website called Massive Science. She stated, *"When predators like hawks, leopards and lions* are around, prey animals, like small birds, squirrels, and gazelles, begin to see their environments as mosaic of safe and dangerous places. Ecologists term this phenomenon the "landscape of fear", and we are just beginning to learn just how strongly hearing bumps in the night can effect animal behaviour". She also goes on to say, "Baby sparrows like most birds, rely on their parents for food. In fact, a 2011 study by this same research group published in Science found that fearful birds feed their offspring less. This led to the starvation death of 1 in 5 baby birds because their parents were too afraid of being preyed on by ravens and hawks to bring them sufficient food".

So according to this article and probably many others, animals do present some type of fear, but yet, humankind is clearly out of sync. Emma Bryce wrote an article called 'What would happen to earth if humans went extinct' on August 16th, 2020, on a website called Live Science, where she stated, "Looking beyond the city limits to the great swatches of farmland that currently cover half of Earths habitable land, there would be a swift recovery of insects, as the application of pesticides and other chemicals ceases with humanity's demise. Surrounding habitats – plant communities, soils, waterways and oceans – will recover, free from the far reaching influence that chemicals have on ecosystems today. That, in turn, will encourage more wildlife to move in and take up residence." It's an interesting statement when you compare it with the idea that if you removed just one species from the planet, there would be a distinct negative knock-on effect, and yet that effect would not be felt if we were to be removed.

So how does all of this relate to fear? Well, I believe that one of humanity's biggest fears, among many others, is change. We are often heavily resistant to it, but I will cover this in more depth down the line. My point is that, if we look at plastic pollution, the use of pesticides on farms, extracting oil, deforestation, and many similar actions, if the reason we do not cease to effect the world negatively is because we are afraid about what our economy would be like if we stopped such processes, if we are worried about our day-to-day lives changing and being affected if we stopped such processes, then it is no wonder why change is slow and why we are so out of sync. My belief is that once we release such fears, it will have a huge positive effect on not just us but everything around us.

Regardless of what theories or ideas I or anyone has, when it comes to this issue, there always seems to be a positive and a negative for holding onto fear. But what I would say is this, I feel it is impossible to see the full scope of our fear because our mind is narrowed by it, similar to how my mind was so narrowed by the fear that I did not see the car in the road or hear it. It is only when we release such fears that I think we will see the full scope of possibilities and understand the truth behind them.

The Dawn of Individuality

Beginning to Question

At the age of 6-7, I went to a primary school called Wattville Primary School and during lunch breaks, after we ate lunch, we would play in the playground like many other kids at other schools. However, during the summer on hot days, they would let us play in the small field at the back of the school. To this day, I'm still not sure why they wouldn't let us play there on a regular basis. However, on a normal hot day playing on the field, I began to have a throbbing pain in my head. Now I'm not sure if I ever had a pain like this before, or maybe I did, but the pain had intensified this time. Due to the pain, I began to have a desire to know why I had the pain, how I got it, and how to remove it. So I asked my dad what the pain was, and he told me that I had a headache, and he told me that I got the headache likely due to dehydration from playing out in the sun. As a kid, I looked up to my dad; he was one of the coolest people I knew, and I was proud to have such a cool dad. Did he do anything particularly different from other dads that made him different? not particularly. But it was because I looked up to him that anything he said or did was just the coolest. So when he told me the reason I had a headache, I did not feel the need to question anything further regarding that issue.

The day that I accepted that answer was purely my choice, and my dad probably learned and accepted the same reasoning as I did when he was younger. At that age, I did not consider if pain was a normal thing or not, but without realising it, I was accepting the world around me and my own pain as normal. Imagine for a moment a world that is free of internal physical or emotional pain. A child born into that world would not see that pain as a normal thing. It would be a world completely opposite from our own.

What's interesting though, is that if you look at emotions and the effect it can have on the body, the results can be surprising. According to Everyday Health.com, Stephanie Cornwell wrote an article on '5 Ways Anger Effects your Health' on February 13th 2024, and this article was medically reviewed by Allison Young MD of American College of Lifestyle Medicine. Without going into too much detail, she goes on to say, *"Experiencing anger triggers the body to release stress hormones, which over time can take a toll on heart health."* She also states, *"evidence also suggests that anger is specifically linked to higher risk of heart attacks."* She later goes on to say, *"Much research shows that the brain and gut are in constant communication and influence each other. One role of our autonomic nervous system is to help regulate digestion. But that can be disturbed when the body goes into fight-or-flight mode, as can happen in response to stress."*

Now, my point regarding this information is that although it is only a theory. If our surface emotions can cause our body pain, what about all the emotions we bottle up for decades, the deep-rooted emotions we don't like to acknowledge? It is possible that they are causing pain too, and by going through a process of releasing those emotions, if that is even possible, we could be pain-free. It is only an "if," of course, but surely it is a goal worth trying for. So when I go back to my statement where I said, "I was accepting my pain as normal," what if I didn't have to? What if we had the ability to be pain-free from the moment we became conscious of our own being?

Absorbing Everything

From the moment we are born, we are fascinated by the world around us. We have this instinctual curiosity to absorb everything we experience. We are not afraid of learning new things, and in fact, we embrace it; our character and personality truly shines. We use all five senses to openly experience the world around us. We begin to love the taste of our favourite meal, the smell of our parents, the sound of our favourite cartoon, the sight of our mothers smiling and the touch of our hands holding a new toy. We bravely learn how to crawl and eventually learn how to balance ourselves so we can walk with the aid of our carers, and we fall down many times in the attempt, but we do not even contemplate our failures; we simply stand back up and try again. The Child is an open book, where the pages are empty but the possibilities are endless.

At some point, we may start developing a taste for music, movies, sports, gaming, and many other things. Typically, most of those things are driven by the people we look up to; it doesn't matter if it's a brother, father, mother, or friend of the family; if they like a particular style of music or movie, we are inclined to like it as well. It is also possible that we may see or hear of someone in a particular field and absorb what they have to say. There are many people who did something special in the world but were originally influenced by others before them.

One example is the legendary Grandmaster Flash, who developed the DJ technique called Quick Mix Theory; he was the founder and creator of the first rap group, Grandmaster Flash and the Furious Five. His birth name was Joseph Robert Saddler, and in Bronx, New York, during high school, he would become involved in the early New York DJ scene that was set up by luminaries like DJ Kool Herc and Disco King Mario. Grandmaster Flash decades later, would talk about how much of an influence they were for him. In a Celebrating 50 Years of Hip Hop interview, Grandmaster Flash went on to say, "*Well, I think, coming up, I watched a lot of DJs in my early teens. And watching the DJs of that particular time, they were playing the music, like, my influences. Although they were great, positive influences – I'm talking about DJ Kool Herc and Pete DJ Jones. These two DJs inspired me to do what I did.".*

Later on during the interview, he mentions his Quick Mix Theory: "*I can take the most exciting part of a record, which we call the break, and sort of extend that, because a lot of these songs that I was listening to were, like, obscure funk tunes where the break section was, like, maybe 10 seconds long. And from a frustrated point of view, I had this thought that if I can just come up with a system, a way of just taking duplicate copies of the record with two turntables and a mixer, I can extend that five- or 10 second part seamlessly and make it 10 minutes if I wanted to. And that's, you know, my thoughts manifested into creating an art form called the Quick Mix Theory.".*

The things that influence us don't just come from other people; they come from experiencing the environment around us. Seeing the stars in the night sky is a wonderful experience that truly never gets old. That single experience has influenced people to venture out into space and experience all the wonders it has to offer. Seeing a bird fly tends to give most people, from the moment they are born to an adult, a feeling of freedom. As a result, it has influenced us to try and understand how it is even possible, and through that single desire, it has inspired the creation of all air-planes.

The World Animal Protection did an article named 'Animal-Inspired Inventions, written by Nicole Barrantes on August 23, 2021, and she stated, "*What do Humpback*

Whales and wind turbines have in common? They both want to reduce drag, a resistance force caused by the motion of a body through a substance, such as water or air. Humpback whales, who can grow to the size of a school bus, can spiral underwater because of the design of their fins. Their fins are lined with small bumps, called tubercles which allows them to reduce drag. When researched at West Chester University learned this, they replicated the tubercles onto the blacked of wind turbines. The result? Studies found a 32% reduction in drag and doubled the performance". She also mentions the Kingfisher bird: *"When Japan's Shinkansen bullet train received noise complaints from residential areas, an engineering team was tasked with designing a train that was quieter and more efficient. Eiji Nakatsu, the Director of Technical Development (who was an avid bird watcher), drew inspiration from the Kingfisher. The Kingfisher is a bird that hunts its prey by diving into water while barely making a splash. They're able to do so quietly because of the shape of their beak. Nakatsu took the design of Kingfisher's beak and applied it to the bullet train. As a result, the new train was 10% faster, used 15 less electricity, and stayed under the 70 dB noise limit in residential areas".*

It comes down to having an open mindset and a willingness to understand all the wonders the world has to offer. Almost like that of a child, a child that does not confide itself in a certain way of thinking; instead, the child wishes to know the truth so they can get a deeper understanding of the surrounding environment.

At some point, we want to act upon our passions and desires; we crave to understand, and so we spend hours, days, and weeks researching the very thing we are interested in. We are willing to read books and watch documentaries on the subject because we are so passionate about it. Eventually, even after some basic understanding, we desire to practice what we have learned and can spend days doing this until we feel like we have a competent understanding of the topic. The legendary musician Prince was an excellent example of this. Prince's parents, John Lewis Nelson and Mattie Della Shaw, both were fans of music, and after their child was born, they named him after John's stage name, Prince Rogers.

In 1950, John Lewis Nelson had made a name for himself in the music scene, and he would play in clubs and community centres on the North Side like the Phyllis Wheatley House, a historic building that opened in 1924 to provide social services for African-American families moving to North Minneapolis. "There were two princes in the house where we lived," Prince wrote in the first pages of his memoir, The Beautiful Ones. "The older one with all the responsibilities of heading a household and the younger one whose only modus operandi was fun." Prince remembers music filling his home from an early age. At his reflective, autobiographical Piano and a Microphone concert at Paisley Park on 21st January, 2016, Prince opened the show by sharing a memory of being enchanted by the sight of his father's piano when he was three years old. "Here comes dad... I'm not supposed to touch his piano... But I want to play it so bad." John and Mattie separated when Prince was just 7 years old, and they eventually got divorced. When his father left home, it gave Prince plenty of opportunities to use his father's piano, and at first he would rely on the melodies from Batman and The Man from U.N.C.L.E. "I can't play piano like dad, though—how does dad do that?"

As Prince grew older, he was no longer intimidated by his father's musical talent; instead, he was inspired by it.

Prince later went on to create 40 studio albums and five live albums, sold over 100 million records worldwide, and was inducted into the Rock and Roll Hall of Fame in 2004.

The emotion of love we have for the topic drives us to understand it from experienced people who can push our understanding even further, and eventually, with enough practice and assistance, we can put our own flair on things. Our personality is expressing itself through our passions and desires to such an extent that some day it may begin to inspire someone else.

The Shadow of Doubt

Even though as children, we can openly aspire to be something and willingly take action to make a dream come true. Sometimes things we cannot foresee get in the way, and without realising it, they can affect us for the rest of our lives. As a kid, I adored Will Smith; he was the guy I wanted to be like. The Fresh Prince of Bel Air, Men in Black, and Independence Day are examples of his work that made me want to be an actor when I was young. I had no idea how difficult it would be or how long it would take, but I had a dream, and that's all that mattered. Even though I had a dream of becoming an actor, I cannot tell you that I gave it my all to become one. At one moment in my life, I was given the opportunity to attend an acting school. This opportunity was given to me by my Nan, who had connections. All I had to do was show up on a specific day, do some improvisation, and be one of the kids that were accepted. The reality is that I was terrified, and I didn't know why. The test to get into the school was simple, I had to convince another actor who was playing my sister to get out of the chair so I could use the remote. One by one, the other kids took turns, and as I was waiting for my turn, I was thinking of what I could say— could I think of something clever to say to get her out of the chair? Eventually it was my turn, but out of fear, I told the teacher I wasn't ready and to come back to me. As the last kid did their improvisation, I was becoming increasingly worried, and in my head, I wanted to be as far away from this place as I possibly could. Luckily for me, the teacher had forgotten I hadn't had a go, but he asked if anyone had not gone, and again, out of fear, I refused to put my hand up.

That was one of the early moments in my life where I realised I had this fear; I didn't know why it was there or how it got there. The truth was that even when I found out I wasn't accepted into the school, it didn't affect me that much because my heart wasn't completely in it; however, I had discovered something I never knew was in me.

The older we get, the more we may face the potential 'reality' of our dreams. We may begin to doubt so many things; the very dreams we held in high esteem as children eventually become brittle and infested with the fears we did not know existed. The countless times I have heard on TV shows and in movies about how some people have dreams of becoming something big when they're young and how they eventually give up on it. I feel like it ends up giving some of us a feeling of our dreams being impossible, a 1 in 1000 chance, and why would I, who may have been born in an underdeveloped society and in an impoverished home, believe I could achieve such a thing? We may also come across such statistics as 96% of adults not doing the job that they wanted to do as children, and only 4% of adults are successfully achieving their dream job as a child. Seeing that kind of statistic would cause anyone to halter and come up with a reason for not even attempting the goal to begin with. It would seem like fate, or maybe we never had the capability to do such a thing to begin with; and so we may adjust our dreams to be what we or others consider "realistic."

Whether we alter our original dreams or not, we may still worry about not achieving them and so we come up with a plan B. We begin to ponder what kind of job I could accept myself being in if what I really desired doesn't come true. We may begin second-guessing ourselves, worried about what hasn't even happened yet. The legendary basketball player Michael Jordan, during his 2020 documentary "The Last Dance," said, *"Why would I think about missing a shot I haven't even taken yet?"* When you begin to think about it in those terms, it beautifully depicts the problem of doubt, which is that many times we do not even try; maybe we do not want to see or feel the reality of missing a shot.

Our parents or caretakers have the biggest influence on us as children, and many times they can lovingly assist us in achieving our dreams, whether we reach them or not. Our parents can also have an unloving effect on us as children, and sometimes without realising it, they may think what they did was normal because their parents or society did it. Many times I have seen parents become fearful about their child leaving them to achieve their dream, whether it means they go off to university or they go abroad to learn something. The issue comes in if the child wants to please the parent. You could imagine how such a need could restrict the child and prevent the child from truly expressing itself. Sometimes parents fear we may be harmed or influenced to do something bad, and so they may tell the child out of fear the bad event that could happen to them. We begin to worry about that and what that could look like; we hesitate and stumble before we've even begun to walk.

Due to our parents, siblings, or other close families own experience of how their dreams ended up and their desire for us to avoid the same emotions they went through, we may aim low. We aim low enough to avoid the disappointment of something that hasn't even happened yet; we avoid the potential sadness that we think we will encounter, the sadness of being rejected; the sadness of aiming high but falling short; the sadness and disappointment of those around you for falling short. Without realising it, the 'reality' of the parent has become the 'reality' of the child. Instead of the child expressing how it truly is by taking actions based on the desires it has, the child can become afraid to act, frozen in fear of another person's 'reality'. So we aim low; in some cases, we don't aim at all; we take whatever the moment gives us. We have become afraid of being ourselves, being how we truly are; instead, we desire to be what our personal fear feels is comfortable and what others around us feel is comfortable or acceptable, and so a facade is created—a facade that hides the true personality from the world around it, a facade that is hiding the grief of its true self, not being allowed to express itself.

The Embracing of Facade

A Moment of Pause

Early September 2005 was my first day of secondary school. I remember my first day to this day. I thought it would be like it was in primary school, where everything was easy going and I'd enjoy myself with the friends that had also chosen to go to the same secondary school. I never knew what hit me. For the first time ever, I felt physically and emotionally smaller than everyone else. I felt conscious of how I looked to everyone around me. For that first year, I relied heavily on my more eccentric friends from primary school to help me adapt. Now, my disposition in the new school was completely different from that in primary school. In primary school, for the most part, I was much more open and not really afraid to be myself. So all of a sudden I'm acting completely different, and I didn't know why, and I didn't even stop to consider why. Over time, I made new friends and adjusted, but things just weren't quite right.

I began to notice things, not just about myself but about others I had not noticed before. All of a sudden, I felt like I had to pretend to be someone else to survive. I had to pretend like nothing bothered me, like I had no fear. I had to pretend to be tough. The reality was that I was somewhat of a Mamas boy; I was soft, I was emotional, I was afraid, and my primary fear every day as I walked into school was that I would be picked on; maybe I would be the one today to get into a fight or feel like I had to defend myself.

The reality is that this fear caused me to skip school some days. I would pretend I was going to school in the mornings, wait for my mum to leave the house 15-20 minutes later, and then go back into the house and be the way I really was—a teenager who was scared and soft, a teen who loved playing video games and watching cartoons. This fear drove me to do three things: either face it and pretend I wanted to do something I didn't want to do; try and hide to see if I could get away with no one trying me that day; and the last thing was to run away and not face it at all.

Let me be clear: I didn't get bullied that often, and only once was I ever physically attacked by a bully; instead, they would occasionally try to reach into my pockets and steal sweets or money. While that might be a light form of bullying, I knew that every time that happened to me or someone else, everyone around us was watching, looking to see what we would do and what they could get away with. It was a feeling of weakness and insecurity that I did not want to feel. Never truly questioning why I had the feeling or why the bully felt like they could do that to someone, on one particular day I had to pause and question it for the very first time.

Outside of school on a weekend, I was walking near my grandma's house, and I saw this bully alone, and instead of him doing what he might have done to me in school, he put up his fist and expected me to give him a fist bump. I was perplexed because I couldn't understand for the life of me why he was completely different outside of school than inside, but it forced me to ask a question. Why? It was asking the question why that I realised, just like myself, he felt in him a need to do what he did, whether it was to please his friends around him, to be liked, or to be admired by his friends. In him was fear, just like in myself: a fear of not being liked, a fear of being alone, or maybe even a fear that others would see weakness and bully him in return.

Still quite immature in my age, I grew angry about the facade of everyone at school, even the facade I had, and through seeing the same pattern, I realised it wasn't just students that had this facade; it was teachers as well.

During an English class, me and my friends were sitting on a round table closest to the teacher, and the typical guys that would harass us on occasion were behind us. The room was dark because we were watching an informational video, and the students behind us were throwing paper balls at us. We tried to ignore it. At the end of the class, just as I was about to walk out, the teacher said the most baffling thing: she told me to pick up the paper balls off the floor, and I told her it was not me that threw them, and she said, "I know." I couldn't believe what I had just heard. The teacher knew they were throwing things but did nothing about it. I refused to pick up the balls and walked outside.

It got me thinking. If the teachers who are there to uphold the learning of the students and take care of their well-being have their own facade and are afraid to speak up, what hope does the school have? You might be wondering what facade the teacher was presenting at that moment. There is one particular possibility, but I do not know for sure, but it would explain the action. It could be that she was afraid of confrontation, and because of that, she may have found it easier to ask me to pick up the balls because she assumed I would be docile about it.

I do feel that having a fear and having a facade are closely related. You see, once we are afraid of something, many times we may attempt to hide it. Thus, in that moment, we have created a facade, a facade specifically designed to hide how we feel from others around us.

Towards the end of my secondary school life, I hated everything about the place; everyone became predictable because I knew their actions were sometimes driven by things they weren't even conscious of. I still had my fears and my facade, so in a way I was being hypocritical; however, it was these moments that really helped me to understand things moving forward.

The Facade

The Cambridge dictionary describes the facade as *"a false appearance that makes someone or something seem more pleasant or better than they really are."* Underneath the facade is our true current condition, not a condition that is falsified for the benefit of others, a condition that may be scarred; it may have some unloving feelings about the world around it, but unless we begin to address those issues firstly by admitting to ourselves truth, those scars will never heal.

Although our parents or environment may have aided in our facades creation, once we get to a certain age, we feel like we have to use it on a consistent basis. It shapes every single one of our actions, sometimes without even acknowledging it. Sometimes, as teens, we feel like we will do anything to be liked, admired, or to seem cool, strong, or even feared. The world around us replicates these same actions; you see it in art, entertainment, or the neighbourhood around you, and so you may begin to assume that this is an accepted part of growing up. Why fix it when it's not broken is usually the term. That phrase is really an excuse to not question or take action on something that we deem normal, but that doesn't mean it can't be improved. And so we follow trends to fit in: who has the newest Jordan's, who has the newest Fortnite skins, who has the newest mobile phone, and those people that don't have those things, we may shame them like someone else would have done to us for not having such things.

In our adolescence, we may have shamed others for being virgins and not having a significant other, and so, of course, the feeling in those shamed is a feeling of pressure or low worth. We may act tough in order to seem strong, constantly needing to seem tougher than others, so we look for their weaknesses, a button we can push because we know we can get away with it. Before we even realise it, this is the world we are perpetuating. As others did before us, we are part of a system, a system that is built on our avoidance of our own fear and sadness.

I feel the underlying fact is that we all deep down desire to be loved. The issue is that in order to seek that love, we may have sacrificed ourselves, sacrificed the very essence that made us. The house theory is full of people who need to be loved or appreciated; the house has no room for people who ask uncomfortable questions; it needs people who are willing to conform; people who are willing to get in line and take action without thought; the house was not created in the interest of our true selves; it was created out of fear of the truth.

Refusal to Challenge

Before we were even born, we did not have an opportunity to say what was normal and what wasn't. Then we were born, and as we grew older, the reality of what is normal began to hit us, and the people we rely on for information, typically also see everything as normal. The world around us sees emotional or physical pain as normal; if we were to ask ourselves now, could we imagine a world without that pain? Most of us probably couldn't. Accepting normality is part of what we do as we get older. I feel some of us do this because it's easier to just agree with everyone around us. I mean, we are just one person. Who do we think we are? "You're just a teenager, so you can't understand anything," they say. "You haven't experienced the real world." So we get pushed back into line, where we try and find what little comfort we can, and because our peers are also "in line," we use them as an excuse for not changing. We may feel Why do I have to be the one to change? Or we don't even realise if we need to change or not. We sometimes see that our peers are not changing their actions or questioning their actions, so we think if they aren't changing, then I won't either.

You can begin to see the repetitive nature of how we operate and the excuses we may use to avoid having to challenge our reality. You can also understand why it is not a nice feeling to be the odd one out—the one everyone points their finger at for being different. For some, they enjoy the attention of being different, and it is typically those that get remembered. Realise that being an individual is where we have the best opportunity to change things. A 'house' full of individuals cannot stand because no one is there to hold up its foundations.

All the tactics we use to refuse challenging the facade and 'house' will forever dictate what actions we will and won't take, and they will dictate our relationships and what we accept and repeat in our adult lives, regardless of our own happiness and freedom. Elizabeth Kublar-Ross was a Swedish psychiatrist, and she once said this about the facade: "*It is not the end of the physical body that should worry us. Rather, our concern must be to live while we're alive—to release our inner selves from the spiritual death that comes with living behind a facade designed to conform to external definitions of who and what we are.*"

Effects of Losing Individuality

Sadly, the more we continue to avoid our emotions and sacrifice our desires or thoughts as a result, the more it adds to the problem. Every time we do avoid ourselves, we add more layers of blocks to our true selves, almost as if we are building a brick wall around our true selves so that no one we know can truly see us. This creates a lot of problems, and the issue is that we do not even realise the problems until they reach boiling point, a point where we cannot take it any more, a point where many people have done a lot of bad things as a result.

Aileen Wuornos was a serial killer during the period of 1989 and 1990. While I understand that she was entirely responsible for the decisions she took, I also cannot say for sure if her serial killer streak was partly because of her childhood. Aileen grew up in Troy, Michigan, with her adoptive parents and her two older adoptive siblings. A fire scarred her face when she was young. She would then develop an explosive temper that didn't help when it came to making friends. Around the age of 10 years old, Wuornos learned that her parents were actually her biological grandparents. This knowledge added more tension to an unhappy household; her grandfather, Lauri, was a harsh disciplinarian who once had Wuornos watch him drown a kitten. Wuornos later stated that she was physically and sexually abused by her grandfather and had sexual relations with her brother during childhood. As an 11-year-old, Wuornos was offering sexual favours to boys she knew if they paid her or gave her cigarettes, which resulted in the derogatory nickname "cigarette pig." Sex work further isolated Wuornos from her peers. Wuornos ran away from home on several occasions, and at some point she was sent to juvenile detention. At 14, Lauri (her grandfather) sent a pregnant Aileen to a Detroit home for unwed mothers. She originally told her family the pregnancy was a result of rape, but later claimed differing reasons for the pregnancy. She gave birth to a boy in March 1971; her infant son was given up for adoption. After giving birth, Wuornos dropped out of school and bounced around between juvenile detention, the Wuornos house, and sleeping in the woods or abandoned cars.

After many years of hitch-hiking and sex work, within a span of 12 months in 1989, Aileen ended up killing seven men. Eventually, on 9th January 1991, Wuornos was arrested, and just over a year later, she was given the death penalty. She was executed on October 9, 2002. Once again, there is no excuse for the actions she took, but questions must be asked: did the many years of sexual abuse as a child, which then led her to willingly commit sexual acts, drive her to a boiling point? At some point she stated, *"I robbed them, and I killed them as cold as ice, and I would do it again, and I know I would kill another person because I've hated humans for a long time."*

It is only while we are at a cliff edge that we begin to retaliate and take actions we never would have considered before. This is typically the case for most people. Even though we may get opportunities to express how we really feel, it is only partially how we feel, and so the mask stays on for situations where we feel we need it, causing more unhappiness. We deep down know the mask is not our real selves, and so we may resent it, resent having to wear something that narrows our vision and grows ever more uncomfortable.

As a result of sacrificing how we really feel, we also reduce our own self-worth because if we are afraid to be ourselves in any given moment, it could mean we do not see ourselves as worth anything. If we had a feeling that "my opinion is not important because I need to agree with someone else's," you can see why that would reduce our self-worth. If you expand that idea into many areas, you can see the result. Such as "what I desire doesn't matter; I have to give into the desires of others," this kind of mindset is prevalent throughout the world. There is a flip side to this though. We can think, "my worth is more important than everyone else's." However, the fear in that case is realising "I am the same," and so a facade was created to help avoid that feeling, a facade to put others down so that itself feels bigger. Both of them are not loving because they are not equal. Whether we purposefully put ourselves down or purposely lift ourselves up above people, you can see why that would create problems, and the truth of the matter is that it has created a lot of problems in the world.

The more we embrace the facade, the more attached we feel to it. It becomes harder and harder to break away, and we are following a long line of generations of people who did the exact same thing. So we walk on, not comprehending the damage we cause in the process. Not understanding ourselves is an understatement; the truth is, even as teens, we do not want to. It is a strong desire to not want to understand ourselves because we know it causes so much pain. It's like willingly cutting out our own hearts, knowing it will leave us there lifeless; though the corpse walks and speaks anyway, the heart is falling behind in the shadow of its former self. Time goes on, and we occasionally look behind us at the heart we once had, failing to understand its original purpose to begin with and not realising the hole in our chest is because of the actions we once took.

I feel that as a result of choosing not to understand ourselves, we turn down our true desires. Going for a desire takes courage, bravery, and vision. It's hard to be brave when we are hiding behind the mask; it's hard to have courage about doing something when what we do is dictated not by our true selves but by the facade that was created out of fear; and it's hard to have vision when the mask narrows it.

We do not realise that while living in our fear, we fail to see what is beyond it; we fail to see sometimes what could be accomplished by facing it. On the 1st December 1955, an African American woman named Rosa Parks refused to surrender her bus seat to a white passenger, and it was because of this that she was arrested for violation of the cities segregation law. Due to this act, the Montgomery Improvement Association was formed, and their initial task was to boycott the transit system and one Martin Luther King, Jr was chosen as their leader and president. He made his first speech as president on the 5th December 1955 and said, "*On so many occasions, Negroes have been intimated and humiliated and oppressed-because of the sheer fact that they were*

Negroes." He later goes on to say, "*We are determined here in Montgomery to work and fight until justice runs down like water and righteousness like a mighty stream."* You see, if we do not face our fears by going after the desire we seek, we will limit our own potential.

During my teens, I told many lies. I lied about going to school when I didn't, I lied about not being afraid when I was, and I lied about being tough when I wasn't. I did this on numerous occasions, sometimes without even realising what I was doing or why I did it; it became automatic; from the moment I stepped into secondary school for the first period, I was lying to myself and others. I sacrificed truth on several occasions, all to save myself from embarrassment or shame. I sacrificed truth to avoid my own emotions and to avoid the potential retaliation of others. The problem comes when we realise it is not just me doing it; we all do it. We are all convincing ourselves that what we see, feel, or hear is true, but I feel we are truly living in a dreamworld that is being held up by each of our needs to avoid reality.

Rarely was I encouraged by my peers, parents, or teachers to open my eyes and see myself for who I truly am, to see everyone else for who they truly are, and to have compassion for myself and others. But no, instead, if we each got a chance to see even a small fraction of someone's true self, we would probably laugh or ridicule such a person. Have we not done it before as a society? How many of us right now are ashamed of a previous action or current feeling and know if people knew the truth? That is the exact response we would get. This would cause anyone to put the mask back on and once again hide and blend in with everyone else, like it never happened.

I feel many of us do not wish to know our personal truth; we in fact hate it. We despise the moment the mirror shows us how we really are, and unfortunately, the avoidance of that feeling causes more blemishes and even more reason to throw the mirror in the bin as we sacrifice the truth we once knew.

We do not think about the expectations we place on other people, the expectations that they help us keep our mask in place and help us repair the cracks in the mask that were created over time. Just like addictions, once the person does not do what we want them to do, we get angry because the hole that has been exposed as a result of their absence feels uncomfortable. We desire to be comfortable, and the reason is obvious: comfort hates change. We cannot be comfortable if what we think we know is always changing. And so we build codependent relationships, where each party has an expectation of the other to help cover up their insecurities and fears about themselves. Even as teenagers, we might hang around with our friends partly because of what they help us to avoid.

I remember when I was in Year 9 of secondary school at the age of 13 or 14, my friends had gone on a field trip to the Black Country Museum. I had already been multiple times, so I decided to stay. However, I didn't realise that all of my friends were going, so at lunch time in the playground, I was there feeling alone and vulnerable. To avoid that feeling, I decided to hang around other students I never even desired to speak to before. They could see straight through my insecurity; they knew I was only with them because I had no one else. Even though I knew that they knew why I was there, I stuck it out and stayed with them for the entire hour. Deep down, I felt like I had degraded myself—not because they weren't nice people to hang around with, but because, for just a brief moment, I got a sense of how much I wanted to run away from my true emotions. Even though they had no desire to hide my insecurities, I knew it was better than nothing, and so I did it. The expectations we have of others holds weight, and that weight builds and builds until we feel the pain in our back from carrying the constant pressure, but what do we care as long as they do their job.

I myself feel that the more we become imbedded in the 'house', the more we lose our individuality, the more our vision becomes blurred, and the light at the end of the tunnel becomes dimmer. It is not permanent; remember, the house is merely an illusion; it was created out of fear, so it feels real. We have all been there, times when we have been in fear, and yet the truth still illudes us. For example, If you tell a person who is afraid of flying all the statistics about how safe an aeroplane is, their fear will still be present. What does this tell us? To me, it tells us that if one day everyone on the planet has no fear, it won't be because someone found the 'way' and automatically overnight fixed everything; it will be because every single individual on the planet chose to.

How We Embrace Stagnation

Seeing the Results

A few years after secondary school, I woke up one day with a desire—a desire like no other I had ever had before. It was a desire to see the world in peace—no more violence, no more famine, no more anger, and no more fear. I knew I could never achieve it by myself, and I knew I couldn't force other people to follow me; instead, I had to be the example, and through that example, they would see the benefits and wish to follow the same path. At the time, I didn't know how exactly it would be possible, and to be honest with you, it felt like it was too ambitious. So the desire felt near impossible; however, I had a vision, and so I decided to try and achieve it regardless of how long it would take. The desire was driven by all the experiences I had at that point in my life; it was obvious to me that something needed to change.

So the very first thing I had to accomplish was to question myself and my own actions, my own fears, and my own beliefs. I developed a desire to want to be loving to everyone, even people some may consider my enemies; I knew that part of loving everyone is treating everyone fairly. Instead of rushing to conclusions and judging a person right away like I may had done before, I had to give them a fair chance, a chance to explain themselves, and even if they couldn't explain themselves, I needed to be able to see it from their point of view.

I will give you an example. Many of us would get irritated if we held a door open for someone and they didn't say thank you, and we might also think they were rude or an idiot. But I had a different thought: what if that person at the moment in time did desire to say "thank you" but was too nervous to interact? What if they were distracted and didn't remember to say thank you? What if they were going through a really tough time and their mind was somewhere else? I had to realise that these were all possibilities, and I may have forgotten to say thank you to someone before and didn't realise it. I had to have some compassion and understanding of the moment. I had to give that person a fair chance and see that I had also made the same mistakes.

In loving everyone, I couldn't play favourites; I couldn't defend someone who I knew was in the wrong just because I knew them. Imagine if you were on the other side of that; you would have a feeling of injustice and would likely try to do the same to someone else because another person did it to you. I had to also realise when I was angry and why I was angry, and that even in my anger, I had to give them a fair chance. It didn't matter if someone I knew had become angry with me or betrayed me; I had to keep the same love for them that I had before the problems occurred.

My eyes began to open as I realised the inconsistency around me and even the inconsistent things I was doing. I remember being at a stop light once in the passenger seat of my dad's car, and as we were waiting for the green light, two pedestrians walked across the road right in front of me. For some reason, although I can't remember exactly what I thought, I thought some really terrible things about them, things I wouldn't say out loud or to their faces. As they faced me, walking back to where we had just come from, I realised they were two of my cousins, and they were two cousins I knew well. Instantly, I had this feeling of, "Oh no, why did I just say that about my cousins?" I immediately realised the problem with my actions; the problem was that I thought it was okay to say it if it wasn't someone I knew, but if it was someone I knew, then I wouldn't have the same feeling and I would think it was fine. The inconsistency was frightening, and I decided from that moment on to try and be consistent with everyone.

Even after having all these desires and realisations, sometimes it wouldn't help because I have fears. I have fears of confrontation; I have fears of other people's opinions of me, and so many times these fears would drive me in the opposite direction. I quickly realised fear was a major cause of a lot of problems on earth, and I somehow had to reduce or remove it, but I didn't know how. Many times, events would be around the corner and trigger a fear, and many times I tried to fix it. The fear was so great that it caused me to feel physically sick sometimes, so I would try to lie down and concentrate to lower the fear. It never truly worked, but it was an attempt.

At that time, my eyes were slowly beginning to open. It was refreshing to see the actual reality—the actual reality we had created—because I felt like I could change it for the better.

Resistance to Change

During a scene in The Matrix, Morpheus said to Neo, "*I feel I owe you an apology. We have a rule: we never free a mind once it has reached a certain age; it is dangerous, and the mind has trouble letting go. I've seen it before, and I'm sorry.*" The Matrix is a movie about Neo becoming free of the dreamworld, and it is in that dreamworld that Morpheus is referring to the mind having trouble letting go. Ironically, this is not far from the truth. We have created a dream world around us. I believe we do not see reality for what it truly is because we do not see ourselves for who we truly are. We have settled in, and we are comfortable.

I sometimes wonder, what is comfortable about it; is it the comfort of living in our own fear, constantly looking over our shoulder as we wait for the next time the mask slips, or is it the comfort of knowing our children will have the same fate? This is it? This is the comfort we scrape, claw, fight for, and die for. It hardly seems worth it. There is an ironic fable that goes like this: if you plunge a frog into boiling water, they will immediately jump out, but if you place them in room-temperature water and slowly heat the water to boiling, the frog won't notice and will slowly cook to death. Unfortunately, this is how we are on a daily basis; we do not wish to change because we do not see the problem.

The term 'ignorance is bliss' is a term I have heard a lot throughout my life. I didn't really have any feelings about it initially, and I didn't know if it was true or not. However, when you really sit and think about it, how could it be true? Logically speaking, the longer you leave a problem, the more problematic it gets. I do not know of many issues that reduce in intensity when they are avoided. Sure, we might initially feel some bliss at not having to deal with the problem, but eventually we are going to feel the heat, and we are going to become more and more uncomfortable. Is it only then that we take action, when being idle is more effort than taking an action? If that is how we truly feel, then it is no wonder we dislike change.

During our adult lives, we often like it when we are as busy as possible because it distracts us from our feelings, helps distract us from questioning our reality, and we barely take a moment to stop and think about why we are taking the actions. We are so entrenched in the facade that we have blocked ourselves from how much pain we are in. The open wounds of our own fear and sadness still fester; they grow with infection on a daily basis, never given a chance to heal themselves. And so we go on; we continue like nothing is wrong, but each time the mask slips, it creates even more pain, but we continue to add more layers of avoidance while we live in the hell created through our own decisions. The sight of our true selves feels like it was long ago, as if we never had one. The innocent child we once knew, who was ready to learn new things with open arms and bravery, is now a shell of its former self. Days go by, but the masks slips still. We do everything in our power to keep things as they are, and so our addictions and expectations increase. What once was enough to patch up the hole now needs much more, and as a result, the sadness inside us increases. Although, on the outside, we often wear the facade of a happy person so that we look like we have everything under control.

In our desperate journey to avoid our true selves, our co-dependent relationships are also suffering because the weight of holding someone up is becoming unbearable. The black hole we feel it is their job to fill is becoming too big, and so we get angry or upset at the other person for not doing what they were supposed to do. It is interesting how in comedy movies or TV shows, when the woman asks the boyfriend or husband, "Do I look good in this?" Then typically, when the husband tells the wife the truth, she may get angry, which I feel is sometimes an avoidance of her feeling low about herself, and instead she might want the boyfriend to lie. It goes both ways. Many times women feel like they have to prop up men's egos, which is really done to help them avoid feeling like they aren't a man. Our expectation is not just that we want them to help us avoid emotion; we also want them to do unloving acts.

The environment around us takes a huge hit because of our choice to be ignorant. If we drop a plastic bottle on the ground, I would assume most of us do not know where it goes or what problems it creates. We may have this feeling that once it's out of sight, it's out of mind, but somewhere down the line, that plastic bottle is going to create a problem for someone else or even something else. Now if you expand that idea into many different areas where we choose to turn a blind eye to our environment and then blow it up to a worldwide scale, you can imagine to some degree why the world might be in such a bad state environmentally. As an example, here are just a few facts about plastic pollution:

- Half of all plastics ever manufactured have been made in the last 15 years.

- Production increased exponentially, from 2.3 million tonnes in 1950 to 448 million tonnes by 2015. Production is expected to double by 2050.

- Every year, about 8 million tonnes of plastic waste escape into the oceans from coastal nations. That's the equivalent of setting five garbage bags full of trash on every foot of coastline around the world.

- Plastics often contain additives, making them stronger, more flexible, and more durable. But many of these additives can extend the life of products if they become litter, with some estimates ranging to at least 400 years to break down.

We can sometimes have this belief that it is not our problem; maybe the laws should be stricter so that we take those kinds of actions less, but can you see that it is just us not wanting to change and demanding others change things around us for us? I remember once, when I was working door to door and I was sitting in the back of my boss's car, he told me to throw my trash out of the car because we had to leave quickly. The problem was that I saw a bin not far from the car, but I had this feeling inside me—a feeling that I must do what he says; otherwise, he will be angry. I paused for a moment and thought, If I throw this rubbish out of the car now, it is only going to create more work for someone who has to pick it up down the line, and so I got out of the car and put it in the bin. I am only telling this story to show the kinds of emotions we may go through and the pressure people may put on us as a reason to blind ourselves.

Just like the person who chooses ignorance for bliss, and just like the person who closes their eyes to their own fear, the problem only becomes bigger. And yet still, we might think nothing is wrong; why is that? It is because, just like the frog inside the pot that is slowly rising in heat, we get used to it and call it "normal." One day, potentially because of our own ignorance, the air pollution will be so bad that we may have to check the air quality before opening a window. We will have to wear gas masks just to step outside, and we will call that "normal."

What we choose to desire is often limited by what we see as reality. It is hard to imagine a future where the world is always happy because we look around us every day and see that this is not the case, and has never been the case. So for many of us, we do not think of such things; we do not develop a desire for that, and so how much we change is drastically limited. We only really change because of a few brave people who discovered new possibilities outside of their reality. If you cast your mind back to the 1800's, no one had ever heard or would have believed an aeroplane could exist—an aeroplane that could carry thousands of people across oceans in just a matter of hours—that too was outside of their reality.

The Wright brothers were the original inventors of the airplane. In 1878, the brothers' father, Milton Wright, brought home a rubber-band-powered toy helicopter. This was designed by French aeronautical experimenter Alphonse Penaud. This toy did not simply fall to the ground as expected; rather, it "flew across the room till it struck the ceiling, where it fluttered awhile, and finally sank to the floor." Though the fragile toy would soon break, the two brothers Wilbur and Orville never forgot it. At some point, they would go on to build their own toy helicopters. Orville later credited their toy helicopter as being the object that sparked their interest in flight. Throughout their lives, the two brothers went into a multitude of ventures, but the one that seemed to stick was the company they formed in 1892 called Wright Cycle Company, where they sold bicycles. With this company, they found a successful business that allowed them time to spend on other projects. Eventually, because of the thriving business, the brothers opened a repair shop and later began manufacturing bicycles.

Though the business was going extremely well, the brothers were growing restless, and two events in 1896 focused their energies: the death of Otto Lilienthal, the celebrated glider experimenter, in a flying accident, and the successful unmanned launch of powered models by Samuel Langley. The business was doing really well, so it gave them the funds they needed for their new interest. The interesting thing about the Wright brothers is that unlike others in the field of aviation, they were not funded by anyone, and furthermore, their bicycle repair and manufacturing company sharpened their mechanical skills, and they would often use the same tools to construct flying machines as they did bicycles.

Confident in succeeding in their plan for flight, Wilbur often took the lead in the early stages, and Orville would soon be an equal collaborator. They knew they needed to refine their solutions based on the concepts of lift and propulsion, but no one had achieved lateral control. They wanted the pilot to dictate where the aircraft would go. At some point, Wilbur came upon the idea of warping the wings, which was an idea given to him by his observation of birds and the idle twisting of a box—to rotate the wings and stabilise flight. They originally tested wing warping on a 5-foot biplane kite.

Their kite was a success, but they realised the weather in Dayton was not suitable for extensive flying experiments, so they wrote to the National Weather Bureau in Washington, D.C., requesting a list of areas on the east coast where the winds were optimal.

Supremely confident in their design, the Wrights built a 17-foot glider with an unusual forward elevator. They went on to test it, but the wings did not generate as much lift as they expected, and the glider ended up flying like a kite. Wilbur's time aloft in free flight totaled only 10 seconds. Although they went home discouraged, they were convinced they had achieved lateral and longitudinal control.

In 1901, they sharpened their focus and attempted to fix their lack of lift issue, so they extended the glider's wingspan to 22 feet, making it the largest glider anyone had attempted to fly, and they increased the camber of the glider. After tests, the lift was still under what they expected, although it was slightly improving. The glider also pitched widely, climbing into stalls; however, they did manage to achieve longitudinal control and eventually glided 335 feet, but the machine was still unpredictable. During the tests, when the pilot raised the left wing to initiate a right turn, the machine instead tended to slip to the left (adverse yaw). This failure brought them to the point of quitting because they realised their work was based on false data. After some consideration, they built a wind tunnel and produced their own data.

The machine they inevitably built in 1902 would embody their research; they gave the machine an efficient 32-foot wingspan and added a vertical tail to counteract the adverse yaw. However, even after many tests that proved this worked, it was still flawed. Sometimes, when the pilot tried to raise the lowered wing to come out of a turn, the machine instead slid sideways towards the wing and spun into the ground. In an attempt to fix the problem, Orville came up with a movable tail to counteract this tendency. After Wilbur thought to link the tail movement to the warping mechanism, the plane could be turned and stabilised smoothly. The Wrights saw that control and stability were linked and that a plane turned by rolling. Six hundred more glides that year satisfied them that they had the first working airplane. In 1903, they would prove it.

The brothers dressed in coats and wore ties that December morning; this was their last chance to prove this before the weather worsened. Words could not be exchanged once the engine began to roar, so Orville positioned himself on the flyer. On a remote, sandy beach in the year 1903, he broke our bond to the earth. He flew; it would last only 12 seconds, and the distance of the flight was less than the length of an airliner. But regardless of the result, he flew, and for the first time, a manned, heavier-than-air machine left the ground by its own power, moved forward under control without losing speed, and landed on a point as high as that from which it started.

The Wright Brothers story is an inspirational one that was created from a vision that superseded our current concept of reality at the time, and their creation allows billions of people to travel all across the world today.

What is our perception of change? I'm not referring to the type of change that is just a slight inconvenience; I am referring to the type of change that would cause our entire way of living to change, our way of thinking, and our entire actions to move from one end of the pendulum to the other. For most people, that kind of change is frustrating because what once existed is no longer what we know; it almost forces us to embrace new possibilities. Many of us despise that change; we hate it to its very core, and we resist it at any given opportunity. So what is the typical result of that? Well, regardless of how much we hate it, it happens anyway, but the result of our detest for it is that change is incredibly slow, and so we stagnate. We don't just stagnate for a few weeks; sometimes we stagnate for centuries. In some cases, we fight change till our dying breath, only for the next generation to bear the consequences.

In our own reluctance to change, it takes us a long time to learn even the most basic of truths.

For millennia, women have experienced many forms of suffering. In particular, it was only 100 years ago in some countries that they were allowed to vote; before that, they had no such rights; in the absence of such rights, they typically had to succumb to the will of men as a result.

Interestingly, the very first self-governing country that granted the vote to all adult women was New Zealand in 1893; South Australia also enfranchised women in 1894; and Western Australia followed in 1899. The woman suffrage movement in the United States began in the mid-19th century, although progress was slow. By 1896, four states had given women the right to vote, and eventually the 19th Amendment finally gave women the right to vote in 1920. Due to this change in the United States, women in the UK began pushing for voting rights as well. Even with heavy resistance, the suffragettes held public meetings, went on hunger strikes, and soon after World War I, all women over the age of 21 were given the right to vote due to the Equal Franchise Act of 1928. Soon after, France gave women the right to vote in 1944, followed by Indonesia, Japan, and Senegal in 1945, and many more countries followed.

Many millennia it took for women to get such rights; the reasons for why it took so long often come down to religious beliefs or cultures that believed women should be second-class citizens and not have positions of power. For example, priests during the mediaeval era saw no benefit in having literate nuns; nuns learned their prayers and devotions likely by memorising what they heard recited, not from reading books. Ancient Rome did not consider women to be equal to men; some received a basic education, and others didn't receive any education at all.

It is possible that even during those days there were some men or women who actually desired for women to have rights. The issue is that we are resistant to change, and so change is slow. The moment we hold onto what we deem to be normal or right is the moment we have potentially ignored what we are doing wrong. I understand that it is possible that if a man in that era decided to back the women of that time, he would likely be ridiculed or physically attacked. It is not easy to do what is right. The problem with not doing the right thing though, is that we are bound to repeat the same negative actions

Consider for a moment that it is likely that during the time when women had little rights, people were completely okay with it and thought it was a good thing. We look at that now and know they were wrong; however, it does pose a question: what if we agree with something or believe in something that we right now consider to be completely normal only for it to be considered asinine centuries later? I believe it is only through questioning our reality that determines our ability to change it.

Support Groups

How do we know what is right and wrong? Do we rely on the government to tell us that? Well, the obvious issue with that is that the laws the government creates are inconsistent, just like us. At one moment in time in the United Kingdom, it was okay for teachers to hit students until they introduced the Education Act in 1986, which abolished corporal punishment in state schools. So if we cannot rely on the government to tell us what is right and wrong, then we can rely on our friends. As I already stated, we are inconsistent, and many times it is the facade we are talking to—a friend who has their own fears and whose thoughts and actions may be dictated by them. So friends are mostly out of the question; surely more experienced family members will have the answer. Unfortunately, some of them have already committed themselves to the dream and will say anything to keep it in place. This is not to say that we cannot learn anything from the people around us, but I believe we must be vigilant and keep an open mind. As adults, we may not realise how much we rely on society, friends, and family to tell us what is and is not accepted. The problem is that sometimes we do not truly have a desire to know, and so what we could know is limited by that desire.

We rely on the people around us to tell us what is right and wrong, so we do not have to think for ourselves. It is much easier to just give that responsibility to someone else and let someone else think about right and wrong so that we ourselves do not have to change.

The issue of knife crime in the UK is prevalent and has been for decades, and people have tried to find a way to put a stop to it. in England, Wales, and Greater Manchester, between 2022 and 2023, years beginning in March and ending in March, there were 50 thousand offences involving a sharp instrument. When you compare that with 10 years prior, it's almost a 50% increase since then. Although the problem has continued to get worse over time, which has resulted in the numbers of the year being just gone, now the people of today see those numbers and the numbers of the past and want knives to be banned. From my perspective, we are not getting down to the cause; from my perspective, even if the number was just one person being killed due to knife crime in a year, that number is still too high. What I am getting at there is that the number doesn't really matter to me. I would begin to look at the cause because you never know if that number could increase from our avoidance of it. This comes back to what we view as right and wrong. I have already stated that we need to be able to come up with that answer on our own by looking at the truth. We have to look at why the people committing the knife crime do what they do. Street violence, fights/gang attacks, family issues, and robbery are the leading causes of knife crime.

Firstly, let's take a look at street violence. It can sometimes come down to antisocial behaviour, when another person's actions make a person feel harassed, scared, or unhappy. If the person who caused the person to feel harassed, scared, or unhappy was more conscious of their own emotions, why they did it, and the effects of ignoring them, in all likelihood they would cease to create that situation because they would likely be aware of why they are doing it and what it leads to. On the other hand, if the person who felt harassed, scared, or unhappy was aware of their emotions and the environment around them wasn't condescending about their emotions, it is likely that they would not take a negative action either because they would not be suppressing themselves. It's the same with any kind of street violence: the emotions are there, but the person, for whatever reason, does not choose to even acknowledge them.

Let's move on to the second leading cause of knife crime: fights and gangs.

According to the NSPCC, the reason people join gangs is due to *"peer pressure and wanting to fit in with their friends. They feel respected and important. They want to feel protected from other gangs or bullies. They want to make money, and they are promised rewards."* Who does that sound like? Do 99% of people on the planet not feel those same things? Do we not want to feel protected when we are with our families? Do we not want to feel respected and important? Do we not feel peer pressure on a regular basis to think a certain way or behave a certain way, even as law-abiding adults? Do we not want money? As a result of wanting money, many of us as adults have taken very unloving actions. So when you look at the reasons youth join gangs, we as adults have to realise we have the same emotions; the only difference is we are not in the same circles. How many of us, during a fight, want to defend ourselves? On top of that, how many of us are willing to kill someone else to save our lives if we believe our lives are threatened? Quite a lot, I'd guess.

The third leading reason for knife crime was family issues. Well, I have already covered that, and to me, it is quite obvious how families can be partly responsible. Robbery is also covered regarding the need for money.

I am not saying one person is to blame; I am not saying the government is to blame; I am not saying the families are to blame. There is no question that a fair chunk of the blame lies in the hands of the offender; it was their choice to take the action after all. But I am also saying that every single person who has the same emotions that cause the events of knife crime is partially responsible. We must begin to realise that, stop putting the entirety of the responsibility on the government for not implementing the right laws, and address the emotions we have all refused to address for centuries all over the world.

As adults, we typically feel like we do take responsibility for things, such as buying a new house and making sure we have enough money at the end of the month to pay the bills. If we have children, we make sure they are fed and clothed and that they do their homework on time. We sometimes take responsibility for our mistakes, and some of us are very keen to apologise when we have done something wrong. These are all great things that we do throughout our lives as a part of taking responsibility. These are all "normal" parts of being an adult. Some of us look forward to the day we can drive a car, have a good enough job so that we can pay for rent, and eventually have an intimate relationship and possibly get married. We have heard stories from close ones of when they bought their first car and how they treasured it; we have heard stories about how our or other parents met; we have heard stories about the moment we were born and how happy they were. These are moments we endlessly hope to accomplish, while possibly forgetting that they are just one part of a bigger world. As long as we are considered valued members of society, we sometimes could care less about what anyone else is doing. As long as everyone around us accepts what we do on a daily basis, we sometimes do not care about the results.

On the subject of us giving other people the responsibility to decide what is right and wrong, many of us have a disposition that closes our mind to learning new things, and so we have this fear of having an open mind because we look at people in the past who have been led astray and wonder if it was because they had an open mind. Maybe it was because they were susceptible to listening and agreeing with others; who does that really sound like? I have often heard that an open mind means you are gullible. Richard Dawkins once said, "*By all means, let's be open-minded, but not so open-minded that our brains drop out.*" He paints an interesting picture there, and it's not so straight-forward to understand. Maybe he means that as a result of our constant open-mindedness, we will become stupid or maybe even lose ourselves. It's hard to say exactly what he means, and I do understand that some people have a very different disposition towards open-mindedness.

My version of it is this. It is almost impossible for you to lose yourself, become stupid, or be influenced if you constantly ask questions. The student in class who always puts their hand up is always the one to learn the truth, and if he has been deceived by the teacher's lying, the student's own will and desire to know the truth will eventually recognise it as deceit and continue on, desiring to seek the truth. A person who seeks truth is not judgmental; they are not prejudiced, and they do not stagnate. Instead, they flow like water, effortlessly moving past obstacles to potentially reach their destination, and even if they reach their destination, they still move, looking for the next cavity to fill.

Who truly influences us, for good or bad? Well, if the environment around us, and yes, that includes our closest people, does not encourage us to ask questions, then we have been influenced to do bad things long ago.

That is the creation of the 'house'. In childhood, we knew ourselves but were slowly forced to accept the "reality" of others around us. As teens, we began to accept the world's reality as our own, forgetting the true self we left behind. As adults, we are sown into the facade, the dreamworld we call "reality," blind and willingly bound. You can place the House Theory in all types of scenarios and see what impact it has, but I first had to show you its creation; only then could you understand its deeper effects in the chapters to come.

John Doe Diaries Part II

The date is... I guess I do not know the date any more; I seemed to have lost track of time in this place. I barely even remember walking into this house, but what I do remember is the feeling of duty and hope I had. It was my duty to be part of this house like my ancestors before me, and I had hoped we would last the test of time and do something other houses could only dream of. Speaking of other houses, what do you see out of that hole? All I see is fog for miles, and it has been like that for quite a while now. I can scarcely see the houses or the street that used to be there; I wouldn't dare walk outside now; being lost is not on my to-do list. However, it does make me wonder what the other houses are experiencing. During the early days of my time in this house, I would be up all day and night trying to make things work. The actions I chose to take over my time were actions the old John Doe would have never considered, but these things just tend to happen. This house... it feels as though the longer I've remained within it, the more I seem to lose myself.

No! I will not sit here and regret the past or distract myself from what needs to be done; I have to take action. I will not be among the quitters of the past; instead, I will do what is necessary to keep this house in order.

Can you feel that? It's subtle, but I can feel it. A change in the wind, but more fierce than the last one. The cold is setting in; we must close these holes before they kill us, and anyone who is not willing to assist must be cast out. The time is nigh for those that remain among us. God help those who stand in our way.

Perceived "Positives" of the 'House'

We helped maintain the 'house'; why not live in it? Surely we can get used to it and find some positives. It is interesting how quickly we can become comfortable in a certain environment. In some ways, it is a good thing; you can almost look at it as survival. I mean, if we were dragged from our actual homes and told to live in an unfamiliar home, initially it might be difficult, but eventually we will have a choice to make: do I run away from the issue or do I try and find some way of living with it? We might take some radical actions to aid in our ability to live with it, and over time we would get used to it, and the next generation that is raised in that new environment would be even more used to it than we initially were. When you relate it to the 'house' in the house theory, we are that next generation. This is part of the reason why change can be slow, we get used to ignoring our own emotions, we get used to other people before us doing the same, and we may try and find any positives we can use as an excuse for staying. This is why, for many of us, we have to hit rock bottom; the most drastic of events has to occur for us to change. I do not believe this to be a necessity; I believe we can change far before that.

I have called this chapter perceived "positives", because I do not believe there are any positives for remaining in the 'house', although many of us do believe there are positives. So, I would like to go over my reasoning why the positives are more so an illusion or just over exaggerated.

Safety

We feel that as long as we stick to the status quo and do not rock the boat, at the very least we will be safe. We will be safe from people projecting anger at us because we are doing what they want. Some of us are very afraid of confrontation, so when things get difficult we may bend and agree with others instead of standing ground. We feel safe from their judgement of us because there is nothing worse than someone we love judging us for taking specific actions, or even society judging us and whispering about us behind our backs. What do we do to avoid that? Stay quiet and stick with the crowd; that way, we will not stand out, or speak up and repeat the things we were taught to think and believe without questioning them.

Many times, we are afraid of people physically or verbally attacking us for going against the grain. Many of us growing up have experienced that as a result of our actions; therefore, we stick to doing what everyone accepts and avoid the punishment. We feel safe when we stick to the shadows, thinking no one can see us, but is that the absolute truth? I feel the reality regarding all of that is that, even when we try to stick to the rules and do what everyone accepts, it is never enough, and so many times we fall short and people project anger at us anyway; many times we may have done things without even realising, completely by accident, and anger is projected at us anyway. In the same attempt at trying to keep everyone happy, again, it is never enough, and so judgement is projecting at us for not doing something right, whether it is judgement for not being a good parent, making a mistake at a job, or forgetting to say thank you because you were distracted. We run into judgement a lot; it peaks over our shoulders, waiting for the next opportunity to strike.

The last one is: do we really avoid verbal or physical abuse? I do not think so; almost all domestic abuse cases would tell you we do not avoid it; it doesn't matter how much we think we are doing right for the opposite person; it is never enough because maybe they want complete control and you even seeming like you have the slightest bit of freedom causes them to attack. In fact, 1 in 3 women and 1 in 4 men have experienced some form of physical violence by an intimate partner.

So overall, how safe do we really feel? If we are all honest with ourselves at this very moment, how safe are we when we are in the 'house', when we prefer to be apart of the crowd? Sure, you could argue that those outside the crowd, the ones that stand out in history, have also not been safe; Martin Luther King and Malcolm X would be two examples, so you may argue what the difference is. Well, to me, the difference is this: those that stay within the crowd, careful not to stand out for fear of attack, are less likely to change things, and so the things we are afraid of will stay the same, and the next generation around you will see your actions and be just as inclined to make the same mistakes. But the person who stands in the spotlight regardless of attack has the ability to be the beacon of light for what the future could look like, and the next generation around such a person will find it easier to stand out.

Avoidance of Terror

We are so afraid of running into the things we are most terrified of. I am not referring to our fears of spiders or heights; I am referring to the fears we locked away decades ago, the fears of not being able to express how we truly feel, the fear of being alone, the fear of other people's opinions, the fear of confrontation, and I could go on. Therefore, we inhabit a 'house' that helps us hide from that fear and surround ourselves with people that help us hide from our insecurities. We tend to do this by not challenging anyone, not asking tough questions, and not questioning our or their "reality." We feel safe from our terror because we feel everyone around us is avoiding it as well, and if everyone is avoiding it, nothing gets questioned; everyone gets to feel comfortable. The reality is that we still encounter this terror on a daily basis; it just doesn't feel that way because we have gotten so good at covering up how we feel or by calling it "normal," and so we gloss over a particular situation.

For example, if we are driving and someone cuts us off in traffic and we get angry, in most cases, I believe the anger is covering over a fear; it could be a fear of death, or it could be a fear of vulnerability. Never the less, we beep our horn, wave our fists in anger, and move on with our day, ignoring the deep terror we just briefly felt. Maybe one day we have ordered something online, and when it is delivered, we realise we didn't get the correct item. What typically happens next is that we get on the phone, call customer service, usually in rage, and get them to fix it. Again, this is likely covering over an emotion; maybe we are terrified of people taking advantage of us. The next day, they send the right item, and we might think the situation is solved; the issue is that the fear we had a chance to feel has once again been ignored.

I feel we are in more fear than we actually realise. The reason why we might not realise it a lot is because we try to cover over the feeling and avoid it as soon as possible. We have become so good at this that, in some cases, it is automatic; I would say all of us at some point rely on some kind of substance to avoid anxiety and nervousness. However, the reality is that no matter what actions we take to avoid the fear, events will continue to occur to trigger that fear. Am I saying that without fear, the events would cease? I do not know for sure, but surely it is worth finding out.

In the 'house' we are not devoid of terror; we do not avoid it, no matter how much we try to avoid the emotion. Remember, the 'house' itself was built out of terror; the 'house' and terror are one, so whilst we remain in the house, theoretically we are enveloped in terror, not avoiding it.

Better Relationships

It is interesting that we sometimes think we get better relationships between friends, colleagues, or family as a result of being in the same 'house', not realising that we are dealing with facades most of the time, and many of us have a lot of needs we need fulfilled. You can compare our needs to a black hole that is never satisfied. We might think we have better relationships because each party is doing what the other wants, and everyone is happy. There is not much to complain about when everyone is getting their needs satisfied. We see positives in them helping us to avoid our fears; we feel like we can rely on them to help us cover up our sadness, and we see these all as positives. We never feel like we can truly open up to another person because we are afraid of feeling vulnerable or afraid that they will judge what is lurking behind the curtain. To be fair, this is not the case all the time, and in fact, some of us have opened up to a significant other or best friend. However, when we don't, we never feel like we truly know the person. According to the University of Rochester Medical Centre, which did an article called *"The Truth about Lying,"* they stated, *"The main reason people lie is low self-esteem. They want to impress, please, and tell someone what they think they want to hear."*

I do believe we have more co-dependent relationships than real ones. In an article written by Wendy Rose Gould on November 7, 2022, on verywellmind.com, she quoted a doctor named Dr. Exelbert, in which they stated, *"Codependency is a circular relationship in which one person needs the other person, who in turn, needs to be needed. The codependent person, known as 'the giver,' feels worthless unless they are needed by – and making sacrifices for – the enabler, otherwise known as the taker."* In the same article, Wendy Rose Gould mentioned another quote from Dr. Exelbert, who goes on to say, *"This dynamic is referred to as a 'relationship addiction' because people with codependency often for relationships that are one-sided, emotionally destructive, and/or abusive".*

Are codependent relationships in the 'house' a forgone conclusion? It is hard to say for certain, especially because there might be people out there who have no friends or family and don't really communicate with anyone, but that doesn't mean they are not part of a 'house', because a 'house' is just a belief that is supported by multiple people. So you can have two people that have the same belief but are on completely different sides of the world; however, once they are aware of one another and their shared beliefs, I do believe some form of codependency will occur. The reason why is because we typically rely on other people. The thought of leaving the house and being alone or questioning the house is uncomfortable, so we remain exactly where we are. As time passes and holes within the belief appear, those within the house must come up with ways to cover over them, and sometimes to do that, we need assistance, and so a dependency is formed.

According to Life Stance Health, who created an article on November 15th 2023, called "How to Tell if a Relationship is Codependent," which was also medically reviewed by Nicholette Jeanza, LPCC-S, it stated, *"It's impossible to tell exactly how many people are in codependent relationships of some sort. But some experts estimate that up to 90 percent of Americans show some signs of dependency."* I am not specifically trying to target Americans with that quote because the reality is that if it is that high in America, there is a possibility that it is just as high or higher in other countries.

I do not feel the house creates or aids better relationships; how could it? If the 'house' relies on the avoidance of a person's true nature, then surely that is not beneficial for anyone. We can only postulate what a relationship could look like without fear or worrying about being an individual, regardless of attacks that may come our way.

Being Loved

Many of us have a fear of not being loved or appreciated; the people inside the 'house' help us avoid that. They give us compliments on our style or our personality; they do what we desire to do and embrace it, even if we can feel it is not truly their desire; they agree with us in certain situations to help us avoid feeling a certain way; and they praise us for doing what we are told so we feel good. We may think this is love, but many times it is based on falsities and insincerity. Remember that Love is a gift and the moment we place expectation and demand upon a gift we are way out of line.

What's interesting is that many times we think we are not being loved when we actually are. If someone tells us we are rude and we truly are being rude, that is a loving thing to do because it is stating the reality of the moment. It doesn't give us the opportunity to go away and make us think we were right, because the truth has been stated, and even if we are resistant to that truth, we can still feel the inconsistency in our story. I feel anyone who helps us remain in our dream world is not loving us, or vice versa. The dream world causes damage without us even realising it; it is only once we awake that we see the reality we condoned. So even in the 'house' we are not loved; being apart of the system does not give us the loving results we might think it does, even though we feel it might.

Less Responsibility

We may feel that because we didn't directly create the 'house', it is not our responsibility to destroy or modify it, and therefore we give that responsibility to someone else. Let someone else come up with all the decisions while we get to lay back and not worry about it. Frequently, we blame the government or our boss for not doing the right thing, not realising that by giving away any responsibility, we have sacrificed the ability to change things. If we want to have any say in what happens, we need to realise how much we are responsible for the condition of everything around us. We may feel like it's a positive to not have to worry and give the reins to someone else, but this is typically how people are led astray. It's like you saying to the driver, "It's your decision; drive where you feel is right," and then when they have driven into an area we do not recognise, an area different from our ideal destination, it's only then that we feel like we have been misled, not realising we have been sleeping for the entire trip.

Everyone in the 'house' is responsible for the consequences of the 'house's' decisions. In a roundabout way, it comes back to the term ignorance is bliss. We may feel that by remaining ignorant, we are devoid of responsibility for the actions or events the 'house' created. I feel it is the complete opposite; by choosing to be ignorant, we have allowed those negative events and actions to take place and therefore are just as responsible.

Togetherness

We might feel like, because we are all in the same 'house', at least we can be together; at least we can have a positive feeling knowing we will have each others back. We feel like we understand each other's purpose for being in the 'house'.

We feel like we can share in each other's pain; we can share scars, reminiscing about the choices we once made and having no desire to fix the current reality. We may feel these are positives, but the moment someone chooses differently, we attack them, judge them, and make sarcastic comments to make them feel bad and hide how angry we really are. The peace we once had is gone, and the companionship we once had has vanished. Did we ever really have it, or was it built on what we thought was real and then got angry once we were shaken awake?

Less Threats

On a social scale, we are sometimes terrified about things being out of control, terrified that the next moment something will change and force us to take a different action or think differently. So we think it is a positive when everything is under control. Many times we feel it is easier that way; it's easier for everyone to wear a blindfold and continue on with their natural lives like nothing is happening until the most heinous of acts causes an uprising. I remember hearing about the story of Emmett Till and seeing pictures of his face. It was almost hard to believe. Emmett Till was an African American boy born in 1941 in Chicago and lived with his mother, grandparents, and cousins in a middle-class black neighbourhood. When he was 14 years old, Emmett left his home to visit relatives in the Mississippi Delta. On the evening of August 24, after picking cotton with his cousins, Emmett went to a store that was run by a white couple in their 20s, Roy and Carolyn Bryant. When Emmett went inside to buy bubble gum, Ms. Bryant was working alone. Emmet's cousin Simeon Wright, 13, and Ruthie Mae Crawford, another black teenager, said Emmett passed money for the bubble gum into Ms. Bryant's hand instead of leaving it on the counter, as white Mississippians generally expected African Americans to do. Ms. Bryant stormed out of the store to get a pistol from her car. Simeon said that Emmett then whistled at Ms. Bryant and that their group became afraid and left quickly.

Four days later, Mr. Bryant and his half brother, J.W. Milam, both Army veterans, abducted Emmett at gunpoint from the Wright family home. The men took him to a barn a 45-minute drive away from Emmett's house and tortured him. The men shot Emmett in the head, tied a 75-pound cotton gin fan to his neck with barbed wire, and tossed his body into the Tallahatchie River. His mutilated corpse was fished out of the water on August 31st.

As soon as Mamie heard that her son had been kidnapped, she began harnessing the political and cultural power of black Chicago. A large crowd was on hand when the train that carried Emmett Till's body arrived. "You didn't die for nothing," she said as the body was transferred to the hearse. The Chicago Defender estimated that 250,000 people attended during the four days of public viewings. The close-up photographs of Emmett's face and body and the television coverage of his funeral turned a local murder into a global symbol of American injustice.

It was moments like Emmett Till's death and the Rosa Parks incident that sparked the civil rights movement.

"We are happy when everyone stays in line," says the oppressor. But then what happens? The real feelings of people can no longer be ignored, so uprisings happen, strikes happen, and everything begins to get out of control. Was it really ever in our control, or were we avoiding the inevitable, just like the frog sat in the pot waiting to be cooked alive.

These are many of the reasons why we hold onto the 'house', why we hold onto our feelings and beliefs; these are some of the reasons we think everything is fine; why we think we are happy but then slowly realise the truth... We are not stable under these circumstances; we are not secure; we simply do not see the rising tide on this small island we call "home.".

How the 'House' Affects Others

We are there inside our 'house', enjoying what little pleasure there is to gain from not changing. We barely see the effect it has on others or how our beliefs or emotions affect people who are outside the 'house'. Yet the people who do not understand and cannot see the reason why we believe in what we believe, the people outside, cannot see how someone can be so blind to an obvious problem, and yet here we are. Who cares if others are affected as long as we get our way? Why should we care if other people outside the 'house' are suffering and in pain because of our actions? Well, imagine if you were in their shoes. You see, I feel we would never try to harm someone if we truly knew the effects of doing such a thing on an emotional level.

Some of us growing up have been physically abused, but we grow up not wanting to do that to our child or people around us because we know how it feels; instead, we grow up with a desire to love them and treat them with all the care we can possibly muster. On the other hand, people might think it is only fair that I harm someone else because someone harmed us, but that thought is illogical because in that instance, you are creating another version of yourself, a version of yourself that has a different personality and qualities, but a version that will have the same pain you have. Now if we imagine what would happen if the person who abused us desired to be more loving, there would be a chance that they would never have abused us from the beginning. This is also where the statement an eye for an eye does not make sense because we both receive the same injury and where does it get us? Inevitably creating more pain through generations, and the generations after us continue the same thing because we taught them the same beliefs we have. But regardless of all of that, here we are, causing pain to other people without truly acknowledging it as our fault or our responsibility. This disposition has created a tonne of pain in the world. Allow me to demonstrate.

Exclusivity

From families to neighbourhoods to cities to countries, we are separated, and sometimes we prefer it that way. In extreme cases some of us do not wish to understand other cultures or other ways of thinking because we feel what we know is best. We are afraid that if we do, they will cause us to change or cause us to face a truth we may have not wanted to see before.

I remember growing up as a child; there was already a gap between both genders. In the playground at primary school, the male children didn't really hang out with the girls, and vice versa. Even in cartoons, male children are taught that "girls have cooties," so don't go near them. My disposition towards girls at a young age was slightly different; I was attracted to them early, and so many times I would do things to gain their approval. To be honest with you, I was afraid about talking to girls because I didn't want to face rejection because I desired their approval, and so many times I would rely on them to come to me so I wouldn't have to experience my own fear. I realised, in my own fear, that I had created a gap between the opposite gender, where they could never truly know me and I couldn't truly know them. As a result I had no desire to learn about their dreams, desires or their personalities; I just wanted approval, and that addiction needed to be met.

The gender problem is a huge problem in the world, and even though it has improved, I still feel there is a massive lack of understanding between the two. This is just one of the ways in which we create boundaries; a 'house' that assists in separation and a lack of understanding of others.

I remember one time in my childhood where I felt I was somewhat close to the opposite gender. There was a new girl in our school, and she was made fun of for her appearance, but I sort of felt sorry for her because I could not see why she was being targeted so heavily. One day I sat by her, and we just talked. I do not remember what we spoke about, but all I feel about that moment is that this was the first time I showed any genuine interest in the opposite gender. We kept on talking and forming a solid friendship; maybe she appreciated me talking to her because no one else would. One day, a couple days before she moved school, I approached the school gates, and there she was. She approached me and gave me a gift; it was a Scoobie toy, which were coloured strings you could make pretty patterns of and tie them in multiple directions.

It suddenly hit me that I had told her I struggled to make any good ones, so she must have made it at home, waited for me by the gate, and gave it to me. I felt emotional, but I held it down. For the first time ever, I received a gift from a girl, not because I expected her to give me one, not because she was a family member, not because it was a special occasion; it was because she had thought of me the night before and desired to spend time making me this gift. Still being a child, that moment never really hit me until many years later, until I matured enough to realise how special the moment was. By desiring to not follow the crowd and verbally abuse her like everyone else did, I discovered something I didn't even realise I had never had. I discovered something I never even knew I wanted.

Sticking to the status quo, we proceed on, refusing to understand another person because of our need to fit in. We go so far sometimes that we pretend they do not exist. It is easier to leave them in their own corner of the world and forget about them. We forget too many times that they are human too and that each human is unique, so each human has something to offer, and by shutting down people, we really are shutting down a whole world of possibilities.

We are so willing to avoid other people and to disown their existence that we have gone to the extreme in some cases and created laws in the past to keep them in place, using laws as a way to avoid our feelings.

Apartheid comes to mind, a law that was supported by the National Party government and was introduced in South Africa in 1948. Apartheid called for the separate development of the different racial groups in South Africa. Apartheid made laws that forced the different racial groups to live and develop separately and grossly unequally too. It attempted to stop all intermarriage and social integration between the racial groups. During Apartheid, having a friendship with someone of a different race generally brought suspicion upon you, or worse. Even worse, apartheid was a social construct in which it severely disadvantaged the majority of the population, simply because they did not share the skin colour of the rulers, and it was created to punish those who disagreed.

Separately, we also hold resources as a way to control how much other people can prosper and create more laws to hold them back, preventing any kind of understanding or relationship. Again, we do this because we feel we are right in doing it, completely ignoring the error. Eventually, the oppressed cannot hold back any more; the wall that was created to hold back the ocean is beginning to crack, and even the slightest crack creates more and more problems until all the pressure we had held back is forced upon us. We are so ignorant that we still do not see this as our fault; we blame them, and eventually we may even become violent as a result of the pressure that is upon us. We still do not see them as fellow humans with emotions; we only see a problem to be fixed. I feel we are yet to see the truth, which is that anything created out of fear is guaranteed to have inconsistencies; it will eventually create problems, and it will inevitably become rotten.

Verbal Abuse

We are ready to abuse others to help us hold onto our "truths." You see, the problem is that truth never hides from more truth. When we discover that $1+1=2$, we are not worried about learning that 12 divided by 6 is also 2 because we know the math behind it and it makes sense. However, the moment we believe $1+1=3$, then we have a problem, because every time we calculate math using that result, it will never make sense, so we avoid any other truth that counters our 'truth'.

We often verbally abuse other people for believing differently and are willing to go so far as to threaten them for thinking differently or for being different, threatening their livelihood or their reputation, all so we can hold onto a belief or emotion. It is a fascinating disposition, one contrived from ignorance, but it is still fascinating. It's fascinating because of how far we are willing to go to hurt others; we hate personal truth, which is our reality. Our aim is to make them feel worthless, and we have numerous tactics to achieve that. Let's start by attacking their character. Maybe we can try to judge them for not being good parents and verbally attack them for some mistakes they may have made. If the recipient feels guilty about something like that, they may well believe that, at that moment, they are worthless. If we need to take it up a notch and attack several people's character, we might try and shame them for their culture or their past decisions that proved to be incorrect. We desire to make them feel bad about themselves; we often desire deep down for them to feel worse than us. We like that; we like having the upper edge; we like being the person on the high ground so we can cut away anyone who tries to come near us. We are terrified of contact, terrified of seeing what we refused to see for so long.

We become desensitised to their feelings; what does it matter if they suffer due to our words as long as we get what we want? It doesn't matter if what we wrote in the newspaper was wrong, as long as we make it look a certain way. As long as we get likes and clicks, we are good. Their emotions no longer matter to us; in reality, that is exactly how some of us feel; we feel as if to other people our emotions do not matter. On a regular basis, we see injustice, we see inconsistency in the world, and we feel the world does not care for us, so we will be the same way with the world. Unfortunately, that only leads one way: repetition. Who cares about the cycle? We believe that if they stop what they're doing, then the world will be a better place anyway, so we choose another tactic: attacking their opinions.

It is interesting to see how people react when it comes to differences of opinion. There is often a condescending reaction to the other person's opinion, sometimes refusing to even look at whether the other side has a point or not. Verbal abuse can be used as a way of covering up our own feelings, just like every other unloving action we take. For example, in our anger, we may start attacking a person's character, but if we weren't angry, would we do such a thing?

I always found it interesting how sometimes, in one moment, you can have friends who, outside of occasional banter, won't say a bad word about each other and wouldn't even think of it. However, the moment either of them does the other wrong, anger and frustration builds and our disposition towards them changes. We seem to have little issue with attacking their character. It's funny because every single time we have an opinion or belief that is unloving and not based on truth, no matter what the circumstances are, the truth always manages to find a way to penetrate and create holes. It doesn't matter how thick we build the walls around our 'house' or how many bars we put on the windows; the truth always finds a way, whether we desire to see it or not. It is inevitable.

Physical Abuse

If things do not change, the verbal abuse we give people is not enough. We feel it is time to take action; after all, action speaks louder than words. We take action and expect results, but what have the results given us? Typically some kind of reaction, an action, sometimes we never saw coming; some would say karma. Karma is a phrase used when someone has been doing something unjust for so long that it finally catches up with them. In a way, you could see the world's current condition as karma for our choice to avoid our emotions over a prolonged period of time.

In the past, we have beaten people who got out of line, bruised them in order to make them realise who is in charge, and fractured bones in order to force them to our will. Some parents have done that exact thing, spanking a child to keep them in line, and some parents go further than that; they don't just want to teach them a lesson; they want to beat the living daylights out of the child. Imagine how much avoidance of our own emotions we would have to go through to get to that point; it is almost unimaginable.

Here we are, many of us, the result of such violence, and what is the excuse? Well, sometimes they claimed it was because they loved us. You can almost see why we all have such a problem understanding love. Other times, it was because they thought it was right. Well, many parents are afraid to hit adults when they feel it is right to do so. Hitting a child is much easier, but until that child gets bigger and we cannot do it any more, then we have a real problem. For some parents, they did it because they were taught it was the only thing to do: to hit an unruly child who refused to do as we told them. It is ironic because many children who go through that grow up to continue being rebels, doing the exact opposite of what those around them think is right. I have known children or teenagers that were beaten by their mothers or fathers one day for being unruly, and the very next day the child does the same thing again.

Parents often do it out of fear; maybe we didn't listen to them about not running off, and just as we did that, we almost got run over by a vehicle, and so the parents spanked us as a result. In that moment, it is likely the parent is hiding in their own fear and causing even more damage as a result. The phrase "spare the rod, spoil the child" comes to mind, as if not sparing the rod hasn't created even more trauma throughout the world.

Sometimes things go even further than that regarding children, and it's not always the parents. in 2021, 1 in 20 children will have been sexually abused. In 2021, there was 694,685 births in the UK. If we believe that statistic to be correct, 5% of those total children born in 2021 will at some point be sexually abused, which totals out to 34,734 children. Generations of children that have been physically abused or sexually abused may eventually grow up to cause the same harm or live in fear due to the abuse. When will the cycle stop? The cycle stops once we acknowledge the emotional cause, but as I already stated, we despise change; we are not interested in personal truth; for many of us, we are interested in blame and repeating the cycle.

When we cannot convince people to see our "truth," we are happy to go the extra mile and get out the guns and knives. Years ago, it would have been a sword and shield, a bow and arrow, and a crossbow. We are happy to advance technology in some of the most destructive creations human beings has to offer. We need to create better weapons so that our enemies have a disadvantage, so of course it has gotten to the point now where countries are stockpiling nuclear weapons. We also desperately need to be at the top of the pile—the one that has all the territory, the one that has all the money, the one that has all the resources—and we are willing to kill others to do it. However, at the very core lays human beings who are afraid, and so the consequences of such fear play out throughout our lives.

I remember seeing a video on "The Case of Michael Drejka." It was a video created by a YouTuber by the name of JCS. The video includes footage of Michael Drejka shooting a man named Markeis McGlockton outside a store in America, and the video shows footage of Michael in the interrogation room explaining his actions. I am not focusing on the interrogation; I want to focus on the act. You see, according to the information JCS obtained, what happened was this: *"Britany Jacobs, who was Markeis' girlfriend, and their three children parked their vehicles in the only handicapped spot located on the side of the store. Markeis got out of the car and went into the store with his 5-year-old son to buy drinks and snacks. About 30 seconds later, while Britany was still inside the car, 47-year-old Michael Drejka pulled up in his Toyota and illegally parked along side her. He got out of his truck and started circling the young mother's car, looking for a disabled parking placard. An altercation ensued after 20 seconds, with witnesses inside the store reportedly hearing a loud and aggressive argument between a male and a female. Markeis exited the store 75 seconds after the start of the confrontation, approached Drejka, and forcefully pushed him to the ground. Exactly 2.5 seconds later, while still laying on the ground, Drejka pulled out a 40-calibre pistol and fired a single round at Markeis, who then ran back into the store and collapsed in front of his son. Paramedics arrived within 19 minutes and rushed him to a nearby hospital; he was pronounced dead at 4.04 p.m.*

Quite a sad story, but I feel it tells our issue with physical violence well. Markeis, for whatever reason, felt the need to push Michael to the ground, and as a retaliation, Michael pulled out his gun, possibly because he thought his life was threatened. It was definitely an overreaction on Michael Drejka's part. However, we have done the same thing: we use all the excuses in the world to take it to the next level, all the excuses in the world to avoid our fear, and someone dies in the end because of those actions.

It is not bravery to punch someone because we do not see eye to eye; it is not bravery to pull out a knife to stab someone because they threatened us; it is not bravery to pull out a gun to shoot someone because we felt our life was in danger. I believe bravery is admitting yourself to the moment, seeing the potential result, and having the guts to put the weapons down. What about the other person's life? We are so afraid that once again we create the very thing we are afraid of, a death, but what does it matter as long as it is not us that dies? Tomorrow, a similar event will occur—next week, next month, and so on. The cycle will not end as long as we are determined to perpetuate the same actions we took yesterday. It is incredible how illogical we can be in the name of fear.

War

I have already spoken briefly about war and its effects. But I want to discuss how, in history, war has been initiated by a lack of understanding and a lack of desire for truth. In order to remain in the 'house', we sometimes must attack those that threaten our way of life or the validity of our beliefs. Any 'house' that opposes ours is the enemy. Most of the time, we do not wish to listen to outsiders because we are in fear that our way of thinking may be incorrect. There is one particular moment in history that demonstrates this the best, and the moment was the Crusades.

By the end of the 11th century, Western Europe had emerged as a significant force in its own right, although it lagged behind other Mediterranean civilizations, such as the Byzantine Empire, which was formerly the eastern half of the Roman Empire, and the Islamic Empire of the Middle East and North Africa. However, Byzantium, over the years, lost quite a lot of territory to the invading Seljuk Turks. After many years of rampaging civil war, the general Alexius Comnenus seized the Byzantine throne in 1081 and secured control over the remaining empire as Emperor Alexius I. In 1095, Alexius sent envoys to Pope Urban II, asking for mercenary troops from the West to help against the constant Turkish threat. Though relations between Christians in the East and those in the West had long been quarrelsome, Alexius' request came at a moment when the situation was considerably improving.

In November 1095, at the Council of Clermont in southern France, the Pope called on Western Christians to take up arms to help the Byzantines and recapture the Holy Land from Muslim control. This moment marked the very beginning of the Crusades: two different religions fighting over territory, fighting for what they believe is rightfully theirs.

It's interesting to hear that at this moment in time, war was happening as often as the sun would rise. From the beginning of the 1000's to the end, there were roughly 50 different wars—that is, roughly 1 war every 2 years—and some of these wars would last for decades and occur between all manner of different countries. The Crusades story continues...

Pope Urban's plea was met with a remarkable response; both military elites and ordinary citizens rose up to join the fight. Those who joined the armed pilgrimage wore a cross as a symbol of the church. The Crusades set the stage for numerous religious knightly military orders, one of which included the Knights Templar, the Teutonic Knight, and the Hospitallers. These groups defended the Holy Land and defended Christian pilgrims travelling to and from the region.

Four armies of the Crusaders were formed from troops from different Western European regions, led by Raymond of Saint-Gilles, Godfrey of Bouillon, Hugh of Vermandois, and Bohemond of Taranto. These groups departed for Byzantium in August 1096. Interestingly, a less organised group of knights and commoners known as the "People's Crusade" set off before the others under the command of a popular preacher known as Peter the Hermit. Ignoring Alexius' advice to wait for the rest of the Crusaders, Peter's army crossed the Bosporus Strait in early August. In the first major battle between the Crusaders and Muslims, Turkish forces heavily defeated the invading Europeans at Cibotus. Another band of Crusaders, led by the notorious Count Emicho, carried out a number of massacres of Jews in various towns in Rhineland in 1096, drawing widespread outrage and causing major problems between Christian and Jewish relations. Eventually, in May 1097, the Crusaders and their Byzantine allies attacked the Seljuk capital in Anatolia. The city surrendered in late June.

Regardless of the deteriorating relationship between the Crusaders and the Byzantine leaders, the combined force continued its march through Anatolia, capturing the great Syrian city of Antioch in June 1098. After numerous internal struggles over the control of Antioch, the Crusaders moved forward and began their march towards the goal, known as Jerusalem, which was then occupied by the Egyptian Fatimids, who, as Shi'ite Muslims, were enemies of the Sunni Seljuks. Outside the boundaries of Jerusalem, the Christians forced the besieged city's governor to surrender by mid-July. As the Christians entered the city, they slaughtered hundreds of men, women, and children in their victorious entrance into Jerusalem.

The crusades had realised their goal; they had taken Jerusalem, no matter the cost. They may have done this in the name of Jesus Christ or God for the sake of territory; however, it is interesting to contemplate the possible mindset of the Crusaders marching on Jerusalem. There is a certain air of superiority about them, willing to cut down children because they may deem themselves to be in the right. There was no consideration for other lives that had grown up in a different culture, most of whom may not have even had a choice to follow such a cause. It is possible that some of the leaders of the Crusades could have been born in Jerusalem instead, following a completely different religion from the one they knew. In that moment where they killed hundreds, there was no room for compassion, no room for contemplation about oneself—unfortunate, really. It is unfortunate that many like them refused to question the validity of their own cause. Surely a God who loves would not want to create a massacre, but these were the times when there was no time to consider what was loving or not; everyone was in fear of something, and when everyone is in fear, everyone feels the consequences. It is moments like this in history that caused me to create The House Theory, a theory divided by multiple people, creating an echo chamber, never desiring to seek truth, fearing the 'house' they believe gives them shelter could erupt, but what exactly is the alternative of seeking truth? A massacre, lies, deceit— it is only those within the 'house' that consider these virtues while everyone outside suffers the consequences.

After the first crusade, there were many more like it, ending in defeats for both sides. While the Crusades ultimately resulted in defeat for the Europeans and a Muslim victory, many argue that they successfully extended the reach of Christianity and Western civilization. The Roman Catholic Church experienced an increase in wealth, and the power of the Pope rose during the Crusades. Trade and transportation also improved throughout Europe as a result of the Crusaders. The war created a constant demand for supplies and transportation, which inevitably resulted in the construction of shipbuilding and the manufacturing of supplies. Among followers of Islam at the time, they regarded the Crusaders as immoral, bloody, and savage. The ruthless and widespread massacre of Muslims, Jews, and other non-Christians resulted in a turmoil of resentment that still persisted many years later.

There is a great quote that was apparently said by Albert Einstein, but it has not been determined, in which he states, "I know not with what weapons World War III will be fought, but World War IV will be fought with sticks and stones." It's an interesting quote that references the never-ending cycle of war and its eventual result, because if the cycle of war is brought about by our greed for resources and territory or our beliefs that have taken us from the point of fighting with swords to fighting with nuclear weapons, the end result will be so devastating that it will send humankind back centuries. But many of us are not interested in others; we are not interested in others pain; we are not even interested in our own pain, physical or emotional; we want what we want. From the moment a sword is swung and the moment a gun is fired, we will continue on, and if through retaliation we have no arms or legs to fight with, we will fight by placing a blade in between our teeth, and if we have no teeth, we will cast daggers at the opposition using our eyes in an inevitable battle of attrition.

The 'House' Emotions

Within the 'house' there are several emotions we can develop or emotions we have that led us to being inside the 'house' to begin with. The feeling of superiority is a common one; it is definitely one of many causes of a lot of problems in the world; however, it develops within us from the moment we enter a 'house'. As a child, I grew up in a quite multicultural city, Birmingham. In 2011, the Birmingham City Council did a census of the ethnicity of Birmingham. The combined total of white people was 57.9%, the combined total of Asians was 26.6%, and the combined total of black people was 9%. Being a kid in school, I saw many different types of people that looked different to me, and although I may have initially questioned this phenomenon, it did not stop me from having a fun time with them and developing good friendships. My father and mother never tried to make me see black people as superior, and so I never saw any reason to see other cultures any differently. I was able to form my own opinion about them without interference, without the emotions of others around me affecting how I was supposed to feel, forcing me to believe one way or another. This is not the case for some people.

To believe that someone is inferior to ourselves is a belief that relies on a village of people to maintain, because if we were left to our own devices, we would likely see the truth. There is no difference, but we need to feel superior.

So the village judges others, not by speaking to the outsiders, at least not yet, but by creating an echo chamber for everyone in the 'house' to hear, for everyone in the 'house' to adhere to, convinced everyone in the 'house' that we know more than those outside, convincing them to believe those outsiders are idiots and that their opinions are irrelevant. Generations of people have to hold up to these standards because their fathers before them did the same. Superiority is truly a dark emotion, and it is only those with their eyes open that can see it for what it truly is. It is a desire to think we are above others, to "think," oh the irony, a generation of thinkers who cannot conceive of the truth; it is beyond our scope, because to see the truth, you have to accept the possibility that what we know right now is incomplete.

Fear of Being Wrong

I do believe we do not like being wrong; we do not like making mistakes. The person who is afraid of being wrong is the person who is afraid to listen to the truth. How do we know if we are afraid of being wrong or not? Well, look at our actions. What exactly do our actions tell us? You see, a person who wants to learn about astronomy does not turn down the opportunity to learn about the subject. However, if the person is afraid of being wrong, what they wish to learn will be limited by that fear, or they will not learn at all. These types of actions take me to several topics throughout the world that I would like to discuss.

About 6 years ago, I watched a documentary series about Scientology called Leah Remini: Scientology and the Aftermath. It was fascinating work she did to tell the stories of several people who were once members of Scientology, what led up to their leaving, and the aftermath of that intention. Leah herself was once into Scientology and eventually left; alongside her in the documentary was one Mike Rinder, who was also a former member of Scientology. In the beginning of the documentary, she speaks about what led her to begin to question Scientology. Leah was a valued member of Scientology at the time, and at one time, she was at Tom Cruise's wedding in a castle in Italy, and she describes a moment where she had a single thought: "Where is Shelly?" Shelly was David Miscaviges wife, who is the leader of Scientology. She goes on to mention that she had that thought because Tom Cruise's wedding was considered the 'wedding of the century' by scientologists, and she wondered why the leader's wife was not attending. She then asked someone where Shelly was, and she got told that it was none of her business to know where Shelly was.

It was her response to that question that sparked her desire to know more about what was going on. Eventually she left Scientology, but she also mentioned how she didn't want to leave initially; she didn't want to believe that everything she had done in Scientology was a lie. It is riveting how it was one pause, one moment, that caused Leah to question her reality, to almost snap her out of what she believed was truth, and she had the bravery to continue down this path and uncover things that she may not have even conceived of being true before, regardless of what the Church of Scientology would do or say to her. Mike Rinder, who, as mentioned before, helped Leah Remini do this documentary, Mike Rinder on the show goes on to describe his endeavours with Scientology; he mentioned how he was a senior member of Scientology, and part of his job was to "discredit and destroy critics who spoke out against the Church. *If the church believed that someone was an enemy and needed to be silenced or destroyed, it was his job, and I did it.*" We all sometimes feel like someone is attacking us for our opinion, and if we feel our opinion is right, we must defend it. The problem is that if we really knew the truth, we would not be afraid of hearing other people's opinions because we would embrace the opportunity to explain ourselves and present the truth using evidence, as long as the person was willing to listen.

In the very first episode of the show, they sit down with Amy Scobee, another 27-year-old former member of Scientology, and go into detail about her life as a scientologist. Amy goes on to discuss her job and speaks about one of Scientology's goals, which was to collect as many celebrities as possible to be associated with Scientology so they could effectively use those celebrities to sell Scientology to people around the world. Her particular mission as a member was to recruit those celebrities and turn them into walking success stories of Scientology. She was also responsible for establishing celebrity centres, building them, staffing them up, and training them so that the centres were perfect. Amy then went into her backstory and depicted how she was 13 years old when her mother went into Scientology and that she got a call from them one day, telling her that they have services that will improve different parts of her life and that they want to introduce her to some of the people in Scientology. She later sat down with a member of Scientology, and the member told Amy that "*she was a spiritual being and that they were in the business of freeing you as a spiritual being.*" To Amy, this proposition sounded brilliant. Amy eventually left school at the age of 14 and became part of the Church of Scientology staff. As part of her job, Amy was out on the streets trying to encourage people to join the church. After she turned 16, she decided to join the Sea Organisation.

According to Mike Rinder, "business *The Sea Organisation is the equivalent to the Vatican or the highest levels of any other religion: the people who devote themselves full-time, 365 days a year, sign a billion-year contract, a commitment for eternal lifetimes to achieve the goals of Scientology. Live communally; they don't have to pay the rent; everything is provided for them, and all they do is work on the Scientology business, day in and day out.*" Mike continues later to say, "*You can join The Sea Organisation from 12 years and above as long as you have parental permission up to the age of 18. When a child joins The Sea Organisation, the parents waive all responsibility, all care, and participation in the life of their child."* Amy goes on to say that her mother was convinced by Scientology to give parental consent. After joining The Sea Organisation, she ended up going to the Scientology International Base in Hemet, California, and she was there for 20 years. Amy later talks about the thing she learned the most while being a Scientologist, which is that the church is always first and that family is a distraction, and the only reason to write a letter back to your family was to make sure your family did not go to the police and file a missing persons report or go to the media because they haven't heard from their children.

Amy was eventually promoted to the Watch Dogs Committee, which manages all of Scientology and is broken down into different sectors, such as the celebrity centre, which she began to be in charge of. She continued sitting down with Leah and told her that she did everything to make celebrities happy and that it was mainly Tom Cruise. She had to surround Scientology staff around Tom Cruise, such as a maid or cook, doing this for Tom personally. She continued to describe the abuses going on with David Miscavige; she was in meetings with him quite often. She said, "He *was a very angry man, and if you said something that didn't please him, he would go off on you, and if you were a man, he would likely hit you, punch you, knock you down, choke you. I witnessed that on at least on a dozen occasions."* Amy later went on to say, "I *saw abuse, punching, and, you know, wrestling around. I would rationalise it all by saying, Well, because we are clearing the planet, because we have no time, and because David Miscavige has most of the pressure because people are failing at their jobs and he is having to do it himself, that's why it's okay that he is beating people. I was rationalising, and my mind immediately would justify why this crap was okay."* Amy later describes how it was moments like this that she became very defiant because she would say things as they were and not continue to make excuses. In July 2003, Amy was sent to the RPF, or Rehabilitation Project Force. According to Amy, *"The Rehabilitation Project Force is basically for Sea Org members who get in big trouble; you run everywhere you go, you do hard manual labour, you call everybody, sir; you have no communication in and no communication out within that group."* Mike Rinder continues to shed more light on the Rehabilitation Project Force and states, *"It's a thought reform programme for members of The Sea Organisation to get them back with the programme and no longer being troublesome, not doing what they're supposed to do, or thinking bad."*

The Rehabilitation Project Force did not achieve what it set out to achieve regarding Amy; she grew even more defiant, and the world she could see beyond the gates of the RPF was nothing like she had ever known; she could see people going to the beach, being with their families, and enjoying themselves. She was scared about the thought of leaving because she never went to high school,

100

she didn't have any life skills, and she didn't have any money. At some point, she met a man who would later become her husband. Although there were guards all over the complex preventing them from leaving, knowing that if they got caught they would be brought back into the RPF, they decided to leave anyway. Once Amy and her later husband stepped outside the gates of Scientology, they were declared enemies of the church. She eventually saw her father for the first time after 27 years apart; however, her mother was still in Scientology.

According to the show, one of the rules once you are in Scientology is that it is strictly forbidden for a Scientologist to have any contact with someone who has been declared an enemy of the Church. Amy was worried that they would target her mother and tell her that she needed to disconnect from her daughter. Once you are declared an enemy of the church, you are declared a suppressive person, and according to Mike Rinder, *"being declared a suppressive person is worse than death."* Amy wanted to speak to her mother first before Scientology could, but at the moment they were talking, there was a knock at the door. Amy proceeded to hide in a back room. The person at the door was known as the Ethics Officer, which is like the enforcer of the church. According to Amy's mother, the Ethics Officer was telling her that *"her daughter was evil, everything she touched was poison, and that she had done so much damage to the church and that she should have nothing to do with her and that she was now a suppressive person."* To be exact, a suppressive person is considered to be someone who is evil and who is interested in seeing people in pain, equivalent to the Devil. The theory is that by stopping the people the

suppressive person loves from talking to them and disowning them, they will eventually realise they have done something wrong and that they will come back to the church. The mother had a husband who was also in science, so she had a choice; eventually, she chose to disconnect from Amy. Some time later, the mother realised her mistake and decided to reconnect with Amy, and that was how her story in the first episode ends.

I respect Leah Remini for doing what she did throughout that documentary, and the change that she went through to get to that point is awesome. The fear of being wrong... throughout that story, that fear was prevalent, and it caused people to do things they wouldn't normally do. It takes a lot of time to hold up a belief that we think is right; it not only takes time, it also takes a ridiculous amount of strength to keep it held, to the point where our arms are on fire and the pain causes us to not even be able to keep focus. By the end, it takes so much out of us that we are exhausted, and sometimes, if we allow it, all the emotion we had held back for so long comes rushing out. It is the emotion we had the ability to acknowledge and feel from the very moment we became conscious of it. It is a shame that, in many cases, it takes decades for those inside the 'house' to get to this point. However, I do not believe this has to be the case; I believe in our ability to change from the very moment we become conscious.

Cults have been one of the most obvious destructive ways of breaking down someone's individuality to the point they become drones, following one or multiple leaders to an inevitable bad ending.

Most cults desire isolation and exclusion because it gives them that extra bit of control they need. The followers become afraid to question anything because once they do, they are ostracised, berated, and ridiculed; they will feel the very thing they are trying to run away from, and so most followers stay quiet until it gets so bad they cannot stay quiet any longer. Along the way, they create excuses to help avoid asking questions. Even contemplating the idea of this group going in the wrong direction becomes terrifying because they know what that means. They may have spent so much time and effort on something that eventually became the thing they never sought out to get.

Ironically, the 'house' has similar themes to a cult. According to the Cambridge Dictionary, the definition of cult is "*a religious group, often living together, whose beliefs are considered extreme or strange by many people.*" The similarities are as follows: Both have willing participants who rarely question the house or their actions, even when things look out of place or abhorrent. Both are typically resistant to change, and even when it does occur, it is only to administer more control, shut down the will of individuals, and allow less truth to enter as a result. However, the most crucial similarity between the 'house' and cults is that they feed off the fear of the individuals within it; it is the very lifeblood that assists in its foundation and its maintenance. Although they are similar, in times past, cults have had much more severe endings, much more brutal than the average 'house'. On one end of the scale, you could have a 'house' of people that believe in Santa Clause, although it is unlikely but still possible. Now, these people wouldn't really cause harm to anyone or at least not straight away; therefore, they would be considered harmless. On the other end of the scale, you can have a 'house' full of people who believe in an eye for an eye; they believe it is an effective way of dealing with certain situations; this particular 'house' could potentially cause generations of pain, generations of people repeating that same cycle.

Regarding the definition stated earlier, this is where a cult is not similar to a 'house'. The people inside the 'house' do not need to live together to be apart of it; the reality is that you can have two people apart of the same 'house' who live in completely different neighbourhoods; they just are'n't aware of each other's existence. Lastly, most of the 'houses' that exist today are not considered extreme or strange. I feel this is the case because the negative impact of the 'house' is often not seen; the negative impact is held within us, and we do so well in hiding it.

So how does this all relate to the title of the chapter, "fear of being wrong," well this is one of the primary fears that stop most people from questioning the 'house'. We are so embedded within it; it has become part of us, and even the thought of letting it go causes us to squirm, cringe at the very thought that we might be wrong, the thought that everyone who taught us what we know about the 'house' is incorrect. So typically, we stay where we are and allow another decade or more to pass by, possibly doing something that is incorrect, doing something that is not only causing us harm but potentially thousands of people outside the 'house' who refused to be apart of it.

Terror of Authority

If you think about The House Theory, the fear of authority is one of the emotions that has to be present for the 'house' to be able to maintain itself; someone has to be leading it, keep everyone in check so that the rules are upheld, and make sure no one leaves. In a family, this is typically the oldest person or the one with the most dominant nature; in a company, this is typically the person who is directly above you, but overall, it is typically the CEO; and in a country, it will be the Prime Minister or the President. Because of our own fear, we may avoid a lot of the issues the leader is facing. Some of us may be afraid because we don't want to get into trouble. One great example of this is Joseph Stalin, the Soviet Union leader.

Stalin was easily depressed when left on his own; he regularly summoned four of his inner circle members to join him for a movie and a meal. Stalin's "comrades-in-arms" at that time included Georgy Malenkov, who was Stalin's likely successor and deputy premier; Lavrenti Beria, Stalin's influential chief of secret police, who was also jockeying for power; Nikita Khrushchev, whom Stalin had summoned to Moscow to balance the power dynamics of Malenkov and Beria; and Nikolai Bulganin, Stalin's defence minister.

Khrushchev later recounted that "as soon as he woke up, he would ring us—the four of us—and either invite us to see a film or start some long conversation about a question that could have been resolved in two minutes." When he summoned a Communist Party Congress—the first in over a decade—in 1952, those attending expected it to outline the roadmap of party succession. Instead, *New York Times* correspondent Harrison Salisbury wrote, "If it had seemed for a short time that the great roles at the part congress were to go to Malenkov or Khruschev, such ideas were quickly dispelled. The great role, the only important one at the congress, was played by Stalin himself."

Rather than chart a clear course forward, Stalin proceeded to shake up the Kremlin hierarchy, appointing a host of young, relative unknowns in positions in ways that were "designed to conceal and confuse the lines of succession rather than clarify," wrote Salisbury. When it came to members of his inner circle, he liked to remind all of them that they were disposable. "He liked to repeat to us, You are blind like kittens," Khrushchev recalled.

"Without me, the imperialists will throttle you." One evening, Stalin summoned the four comrades to watch a movie together. Afterwards, they retired to Stalin's Kuntesvo dacha, where they sat down and enjoyed a meal, during which Stalin inquired whether confessions had been extracted for a trial he would soon oversee. That winter, Stalin had been waging a witch hunt against Kremlin physicians, many of whom were Jewish, claiming they murdered top Soviet officials in a "doctors" plot. The trial against the Kremlin doctors was to commence within weeks.

According to Khrushchev's account of the night, they finished around 5 or 6 in the morning. "We said goodbye to Comrade Stalin and departed," he wrote. "I remember that when we were in the entrance hall, Stalin came out as usual to see us off. He was in a jocular mood and joked a lot. He waved his index finger or his first and prodded me in the stomach, calling me Mikola. He always used the Ukrainian form of my name when he was in good spirits. Well, we left in good spirits too, since nothing had happened during the dinner. Those dinners did not always end on a happy note."

The next day, a Sunday, Khrushchev says he remained at home, expecting Stalin to call to extend an invitation for that evening. But Stalin did not call him, or anyone else for that matter. He didn't ring for food, nor had the sensors installed in Stalin's rooms detected movement.

According to later interviews, those working at the dacha claimed they were too scared to disturb Stalin. It took until around 10:30 at night for someone to check on Stalin. According to one account, one of the guards, Peter Lozgachev, was the one who finally entered Stalin's quarters, ostensibly to drop off official mail from the Kremlin. Other accounts say it was the long-time maid. Whoever entered the room found the dictator on the ground in his pyjamas, the floor soaked with urine. An empty glass and mineral water were on the table, and it appeared as though Stalin had gotten out of bed to get water but then had a stroke. At some point, the staff at the dacha contacted the four members. Beria and Malenkov arrived first at the dacha. According to testimony compiled by Miguel A. Faria in the journal *Surgical Neurology International*, Lozgachev said that Beria, upon seeing Stalin snoring, asked, "Lozgachev, why are you in such a panic? Can you see that Comrade Stalin is sleeping soundly? Don't disturb him and stop alarming us." Even if no one had poisoned Stalin the night before, Simon Sebag Montefiore in *Stalin: The Court of the Red Tsar* suggested they could have observed the state he was in and made a decision there to hasten his death. Signs pointed to Beria having fallen out of Stalin's good graces, and thus he potentially stood to gain the most from the leader's death. But Beria could have also believed what he was saying; to an untrained eye, Stalin may very well have appeared to be sleeping. And with the doctors plot trial commencing in the coming weeks, no one wanted to have to be the one to call a doctor. "The inner circle was so accustomed to his minute control that they could barely function on their own," Montefiore added.

Intentionally or not, it took until around 7 in the morning for all four of his members to reach a decision, which was to call the Minister of Health to select doctors to take an initial look at Stalin. When the doctors arrived, they found Stalin unresponsive, his right arm and leg paralysed, and his blood pressure at an alarmingly high rate of 190/110. "They had to examine him, but their hands were too shaky. To make it worse, the dentist took out his dentures and dropped them by accident," according to Lozgachev's testimony. They ordered complete silence, put leeches behind his ears, put a cold compress on his head, and recommended he not eat. Two days after the doctors first saw him, Radio Moscow made the announcement, revealing Stalin had suffered a stroke on Sunday night.

The events surrounding Stalin's death are certainly interesting; the fear he imposed on everyone around him made things quite difficult. Fear has been used as a tactic to control people for centuries, and you can understand why it is so effective. We struggle many times to look past our fear; it's like running into a brick wall; it's almost impossible to see what future lies behind it, so we either stay there and be stagnant, become angry, and start hitting the wall, which only causes ourselves damage, or we run away to what we are comfortable with. When the option of running away or fighting is not possible, we feel like we have to remain there, doing what the fear demands of us. You see, the possibility of releasing fear was never considered; many of us do not even think it is possible, so we do not try. Remaining in the terror of authority only to become a victim of the inevitable harsh reality we end up creating for ourselves.

How the 'House' Affects us Personally

Years and years go by, and we have walked for so long without direction that we do not even recognise our surroundings. We think of moments of what it was like when we were young and how we had less pain. We begin to reminisce about "the good ol' days," not quite remembering how we really felt at that time. Our memory begins to fade about our past; some of what we have done has long since been thrown under the carpet, never to be seen again. Not realising that as a result of such actions, we cannot see the horizon any more, our past pain and hurt have blocked our ability to see beyond ourselves. In some cases, when we are walking with no direction, we begin to feel angry, which is our way of still refusing to feel our sadness about moments from the past.

It is interesting to hear us talk about what our lives mean up to this point. Many of us feel like we are just waiting for the clock to run down, waiting for that last heartbeat. Some of us may feel like we will go to heaven or an equivalent, and everything will be alright—no more pain. However, no matter which way you think, we are all trying to run away from the responsibility of the actions we once took and the effects that had on our being and the people around us. It's the job of the next generation to fix the errors created or assisted, and the next generation after that. The problem is that if the next generation follows our lead, they will have the same emotional pain, make the same mistakes, and feel the same way we do right now. I feel everyone has the ability right now to look at what the effects the 'house' has on them personally and to correct that, so the next generation can follow behind.

Anger is but one such effect. We are angry because we have done what other people wish us to do, and it never feels like enough, so we feel like we have wasted our time and wasted the potential of what could have been. We are angry because the society around us demands so many things from us, and the longer we go on, the more we feel it day in and day out. A feeling of needing to smile when we take a picture even though we are raging inside, a feeling that no matter how we feel, we must stick with the protocol. It is tiring; we are tired of doing the same thing without seeing any significant improvement, and we realise that our "reality" is not what we thought it was going to be. It is interesting when you see people who have won the lottery—the people who once had very little all of a sudden get something they have been dreaming of for years. Money is now in their grasp, and all the things they desire are likely to come true.

Jason and Victoria Jones were one such example when they celebrated winning $2.3 million back in 2004. The couple had only been married for a year when they won the lottery. However, 12 years later, they said the fortune had ruined their lives, despite owning a luxury home, a sports car, and an impressive property portfolio in Devizes, Wiltshire. They eventually split in 2016, with

Victoria speaking quite frankly about the stress. She said, *"It's probably one of the worst things that's ever happened to me. Without a shadow of a doubt."* She also went on to say, *"The stress it gives you in life, and even 12 years down the line, I'm still classified as a lottery winner, and it's horrible. It ruins your life. People treat you differently; it's just not a nice thing"*.

We often feel like nothing is ever good enough, and the truth is, it doesn't matter how much money we have or how many possessions we hold; the sadness we feel deep down does not go away; instead, it grows over time. We make new goals, thinking it will fix itself once we get there, but we are still unwilling to recognise the real problem. Our reality is not the blissful dream we once thought it was, and the anger of having to feel the reality of that is weighing on us. We may get this sense that life is unfair and begin to look at others, thinking the grass is greener, thinking "surely his or her life is better than my own," and we desire to be someone else or something else, still running away from the reality we had a part in maintaining and are still maintaining to this day. We may feel like we have been misled because we must have gotten here somehow, and it cannot be our fault. This "reality" is not what we had desired for ourselves; it was meant to be easier; it was meant to be happier; surely someone is to blame.

So who do we get angry at? Maybe our parents are to blame because they brought us up; they told us what we were going to get as a reward, but instead all we feel is more anger and sadness, and our fears are more prominent. Many males, when they were younger, were told by others not to show emotion. Emotion makes men look weak, so we don't even mention it, allowing it to fester because of the negative connotation we and other people had about men being emotional. Separately, we begin to think about all the times our parents might not have loved us, all the times we may have hated them for hitting us, shouting at us, blaming us, and judging us, and in some ways, even though we are adults now, we still feel like children, stuck in that moment in time where we felt fear of our parents, stuck in a time where we were not allowed to be ourselves.

But is it truly all their fault? Are we not adults now? Do we not have a responsibility to take control of the reality we helped to maintain, a reality we may have forced other people to adhere to, a reality we mocked and ridiculed other people to believe in and condemned those who chose not to? Yes, we are that person. The anger we hold towards society because of the reality we live in—a society we once thought was credible and stood for something no longer does. But what exactly did it stand for—the freedom of others? The happiness of others? Nope, because no one truly feels free or happy. It is only then that we realise I am the result of what I once stood for. I stood for all the emotion and physical pain we endured willingly. I am the person who stood for our stagnation, and I am the one who stood to make sure it was never questioned. Society is made up of people, ruled by the Council, a Prime Minister, or a President. Yes, but it is the people who truly rule it. Not by force but by our willing desire to see what is wrong and change what is in front of us. If we do not change well, then nothing does.

We hold resentment towards the world for being the way it is; we feel it is not the world we once remembered. We may feel the youth are different from how we were as kids; the women were different, and the men were different. We might even feel like what we once had was the right way to do things, again not realising we had a hand in creating this and that things must change. Each generation changed based on the environment it was in; for example, computers are much more widely available now than they were 20 years ago, and the reason is understandable. The percentage of homes in the UK that had a personal computer was just 17% in 1990, and in 2018, the percentage drastically increased to 88% (Statista, 7 December 2020). whether it is a smart watch or a tablet. Times have changed, and so has the generation. The only things that have refused to change are the emotions, the emotions that were in the generation before them, and the techniques we use to not challenge them.

The resentment grows to the point that our faces cannot hold up the mask any longer, and on top of other people, everyone inside the 'house' is to blame; the people we thought were on the same side as us start turning against each other. We cannot hold back any longer, and so arguments ensue; we cannot tell any more lies; the truth must finally be revealed; and the valve must burst open after holding the pressure back for so long. All the details we have kept in the back of our minds on days like this—days where we can tell people how we really feel and hold what we know against them—of course they have been doing the same thing, and so it becomes a verbal war, one bomb after another.

We are in such a rage that neither of us can recognise the other any more, and all we can think about is how much the other person is wrong, how much of an idiot they are, and how much we hate them. It is only when our emotions calm down that we think we may have gone too far and that our actions have been irrational, or we could take it even further. Our desire to take it even further boils over into violence; the same people we were breaking bread with 24 hours ago are the same people we are fighting today. The avoidance of all our emotions has driven us to this point. No, it was not one event that triggered the brawl; it was one event that was the straw that broke the Camels back.

Years and years of avoidance techniques were used to get to this moment, a moment where we feel like we cannot even communicate any more because, to be honest, even when we did communicate before, we were not truly being ourselves and expressing ourselves to the other person, whoever that person may be. It is fascinating to hear society's opinion on violence between friends, family, or colleagues. The author Jane Corry once said,

"Love is close to hate when it comes to sisters. You're as close as two humans can be. You came from the same womb and the same background. Even if you're poles apart mentally, That's why it hurts so much when your sister is unkind. It's as though part of you is turning against yourself.".

We often feel like fighting between siblings, family, friends, and so on is a part of life and we should accept it because it is sometimes going to happen, rarely desiring to recognise the true cause behind each person's actions. Many people feel this way, and so many people fight as a result. People may feel like that is a form of love and that the hate we may harbour for each other should not be addressed, as if there is no other way to let out the hate without a good scrap every now and again. Generations of people have taught us it is not possible, but does that mean we should not try? I'm sure 500 years ago, men and women thought humans landing on the moon was impossible; many of them back then couldn't even envisage video calling. Right now, many of us do not envisage a world that has no fighting in it; does that mean it is not possible?

Lack of Emotional Responsibility

Recently, I have come to the conclusion that many of us, if not all of us, do not take emotional responsibility for the world around us, and we instead only attempt to deal with the effects and assume it has nothing to do with us personally.

We see so many chaotic events throughout the world and put all the blame directly on the person or people who committed them. We never stop to think, How have I contributed to the problem? Am I to blame as well? What have I done to help create the problem? We do not realise how much our own emotions affect those around us and what avoiding those emotions does to them.

I will use the Theranos example. Theranos was a company founded in 2003 by Elizabeth Holmes. Her aim was to revolutionise blood testing. In 2004, Theranos raised $6.9 million in early funding, gaining a valuation of $30 million. The company's valuation continued to rise as it gained more funding, eventually hitting $9 billion, and Holmes effectively became a billionaire because of her 50% stake in the company. Despite the company's big valuation, Holmes wouldn't talk about how exactly Theranos' technology worked, and the technology had never been submitted for peer review in medical journals. According to the American National Library of Medicine website, "*a peer review is intended to serve two primary purposes. Firstly, it acts as a filter to ensure that only high-quality research is published, especially in reputable journals, by determining the validity, significance, and originality of the study. Secondly, peer review is intended to improve the quality of manuscripts that are deemed suitable for publication.*". Almost a year later, The Wall Street Journal ran a scathing article criticising Theranos, and Theranos supplied over 1,000 pages of documentation to refute the allegations. A few months later, a $350 million deal with Safeway fizzled out after Theranos failed to meet key deadlines for rollouts and Safeway executives questioned the validity of test results.

After years of bad press, being maligned by other companies in the industry, and settling fraud lawsuits from large investors, on March 14, 2018, the SEC charged Theranos, its founder and CEO Elizabeth Holmes, and its former President Ramesh "Sunny" Balwani with massive fraud. The federal grand jury indicted both Holmes and Balwani on nine counts of wire fraud and two counts of conspiracy to commit wire fraud. The press release from the U.S. Attorney's Office stated that in order to promote Theranos, both Holmes and Balwani "*engaged in a multi-million dollar scheme to defraud investors and a separate scheme to defraud doctors and patients.*". Elizabeth Holmes was convicted on 4 out of 11 federal charges for conspiring to defraud investors. She would ultimately be sentenced to 11 years and 3 months in prison. Balwani, six months later, was found guilty of all charges and ultimately sentenced to nearly 13 years in prison.

According to EQS Integrity Line, which is a website that did an extensive blog on Theranos and wrote, "*Many times during Theranos' day employees in the laboratory drew attention to the problems with "Edison," which was the machine created to test blood. The companies would document error reports. Those tips were ignored by company management. Instead of working on a solution to the problem, only the correct data was filtered out of the results of the test runs in the company and further evaluated. The wrong results were ignored. Balwani allegedly pressured doubting or critical employees*". Former staff members describe the Theranos company culture as a mixture of distrust, psychological pressure, and lies. Numerous employees resigned or were fired if they asked too many questions or were too critical. According to CNN, a former employee stated, "*I think a lot of us were in denial.*" Another employee said, "*They really did keep people in their own little bubbles.*" Many employees struggled to find work after Theranos; one employee said, "*I took off six months after the layout to get over this.*" She went on to say, "*I was exhausted, emotionally and physically.*".

The reason why I used the Theranos example is because it is an example of many other instances in which people decided to take action even though they were lying to themselves and investors, and they knew the long-term consequences if they were ever found out. So how is everyone else involved? How am I the person who sat at home watching it on the news and had nothing to do with the company involved? Well, the answer is simple: how many of us have avoided telling the truth to avoid another person's actions, in order to avoid a person shouting at us, laughing at us, fighting us, or firing us? You see, many of the employees at Theranos had the same emotions. Many of them were also afraid of being fired because they were worried about not being able to pay bills, not being able to feed themselves or their children, and they were worried they may not get another job.

Fear is at the cause of this, so if we have the same emotions, how do we know we wouldn't have taken the same actions? How do we know we wouldn't have sat there and done nothing? It is only then that you can begin to have some compassion for the employees of the company because we see the bigger picture. Even in Elizabeth's case, she may have had the exact same fears; maybe she was afraid of admitting the truth, and everyone around her thinking that she was a fraud, projecting anger and hatred towards her due to her actions. Due to this fear, she could become to be in denial, and in this denial, she would berate anyone around her who began to ask deeper questions. She may threaten and fire people because of that fear. Now, truly, how many of us would also be afraid? Many of us are in denial right now, and we do not wish to see it. There is no excuse for what she did, but maybe if she knew people were more compassionate and understanding, she would have come clean sooner. We tend to feel like being aggressive or angry at someone doing something wrong will cause other people to not do it, but it has a completely different effect; it causes people to be afraid of taking action. On the other hand, if the employees were not afraid, maybe Theranos would not have gotten as far as it did.

These are the things we must think about, and this is just one example. We must see how our reactions to the truth affect whether or not people will tell the truth in the future. We have to see how the excuses to avoid our own emotions cause everyone around us to create the same excuse and do the same thing. Again, this was just one example, but how many other examples can we think of? How many other events in history were caused by the emotions we still hold onto today?

The future is in jeopardy; the same emotions that caused problems yesterday may also cause more problems tomorrow. We often look at individual events and think, "Well, at least it is over." But it is not truly over, but we convince ourselves it is over anyway because it is easier that way. it is easier to just blame someone else and move on until the next event is created, and it is only then that we realise nothing has really changed. The events we once thought could never happen again has happened, and we have collectively created another event similar to the last one.

I remember hearing about the cane toad infestation in Australia.

In the 1930's, Australia's northern sugar cane industry was facing an enormous population of cane beetles, which were eating away at the crops. Despite the possibility of environmental impact, the industry was placing great pressure on political figures and won out in 1935, which successfully allowed them to bring in the Central American cane toad as a form of biological control. The hope was that the cane toad would end up eating the cane beetles and keeping the sugar cane intact, which would eventually solve the pest problem. It was a successful case study to work off, and an article at the time named 'Toads Save Sugar Crop', hailed their triumphant introduction as pest control in Puerto Rico.

However, unlike Puerto Rico, the cane toads that we brought to Australia were a complete failure, not because the cane toads weren't eating the beetles, but because they also ate other species within the area as they left the dry open fields for more plentiful food in diverse areas. They feasted on unintended insects, like ants that consume cane beetle larvae, which inevitably cancelled out some of their intended pest control benefits. But the issue was not only due to what the toads ate, but instead what ate them. Large native species that eat cane beetles, lizards, and goannas started to eat the cane toads and suffered poisoning from the toxic glands on the toad's backs. Another issue was that rats, which ate the cane toads and the valuable sugar cane, thrived. Rats were unfortunately one of the few species immune to the cane toad's toxins and increased in number, while the predators of rate, such as goannas, suffered population declines. Overall, the cane toads thrived, while the cane beetle population essentially went unchanged.

The number of cane toads boomed in Australia; where there were initially just a few thousand, there are now over 200 million. Due to this increased number, it accompanied rapid evolutionary developments, including longer legs on toads found at the frontier as their territories expanded at approximately 60 km per year. The species also developed cannibalistic tendencies in this short span of time, likely due to their large numbers and lack of predators, which leads to a competition for resources.

It wasn't just the toads that were making evolutionary changes. Crows and kites are known to turn cane toads over onto their backs to avoid contact with their poisonous glands, leaving the skin uneaten. Australia's otters (known as Rakali) use surgical precision to avoid the toad's toxic organs.

Since then, cane toads have been named by National Geographic as one of the most damaging invasive species in the world. Reports by the Australian government conclude that the eradication of the species is unlikely and that some of its damage is irreversible.

The avoidance of fear is the problem, event after event, and we still do not see that, and so our future is compromised before it has even begun. In regards to the industry that brought in the cane toads, the fear was clear; they were afraid of losing their crop. We are so desperate to hang on to what we think we know, to the dream, to the house that we use to avoid our fear, and it is because of that that we create the very thing we are afraid of. Imagine where we could be as humans if we challenged our reality from the moment it was created and what the environment we live in could look like. It is only once we face that fear that we can begin to see the future and all its possibilities. A world event such as war is usually created by the collective avoidance of fear. Its sometimes not only fear but also greed, selfishness, and superiority—many of these emotions many people harbour even to this day.

If we all have the same fears, then we could not only affect whether or not a country goes to war, but we could also accept it. It is truly saddening that millions of people die in war. Even the people who are not soldiers or commanders are affected; the whole world is affected, and instead of taking emotional responsibility for what each of us has done, we are quick to point the finger and think, "If you get rid of this person, the problem goes away." No, it will not.

What is a hero to you? When we say the word "hero," we begin to think of Spider-man or Superman saving the day and protecting people from the bad guys. I believe we are all the result of the reality we helped to create and maintain; we are victims of our own actions. A true hero is someone who has the courage to say the truth, no matter the consequences. Some of the bravest men and women in history have done that exact thing and sometimes died for it as a consequence, but no matter the consequence, it is the truth that has always pushed mankind forward, and it is true heroes that understand that.

Grief Over Truth

After spending so much of our time avoiding the truth, the truth about how we feel about ourselves, the truth about how we feel about what actions we took and why. Deep down, there is sadness; grief is the better word for it. We feel there is something wrong, and we know it, but yet we do nothing about it anyway. It is that grief that, deep down we all feel. How would many of us feel if tomorrow we learned the truth about all our physical pain and that we no longer needed to suffer it? While yes, we would feel joyous, you can understand that we would think about all the times in which we sat there in pain, all the times we told our children they had to sit in it too, all the money we spent avoiding pain was a waste of money, and that it was never necessary to begin with.

Imagine we are on an island, and we have never known other land. To set the scene, the island is not in great condition; it is quite small but large enough for you to stay on. There is not much vegetation, and every now and then the tide becomes so high that it covers most of the island, leaving us in the centre of it feeling trapped and alone. Now, our disposition to this situation changes depending on the person. Many of us would feel like we are stuck here, and we must make the best of what we have. Some would use their imagination and think of an island out there beyond the horizon that has everything we need. Imagine that, out of our own fear, we stay on that island, malnourished and terrified, and we stay there for decades. But one day we grow the courage to build a raft so it can carry us out onto better land. Eventually, we see land, and it is unlike anything we could have imagined, and it has all the things we require. In that moment, we might call ourselves stupid for not coming here sooner; we wouldn't have starved for so many years, and the grief of realising we chose to stay there begins to hit us.

That grief is there because we know there is a truth out there that is better for us, but we are not brave enough to reach for it. Sometimes we cannot even imagine it, but the feeling is there anyway, knocking at our door. Even though, through our denial, we cannot hear the knock, we feel its vibration permeating throughout the house.

We avoid the truth because we feel like we will lose what we know. Some of us feel like we have a great relationship with our parents, so even just contemplating the thought that the relationship might not be as good as we thought or that maybe they didn't love us as much as we thought growing up is terrifying. If we tell our parents how we really feel, maybe they won't like us any more. If I change my actions, I won't be able to do the things I enjoy any more. We think about these things automatically sometimes and automatically take actions; we rarely stop to think about what we could gain; maybe if I'm truthful, people around me will be more open, and each party feels they can tell us how they truly feel without having to hold it in. The reality is that we might not like what we hear, but only then can we see the true person and potentially have a true relationship. So what exactly are we losing? We are not losing ourselves because we haven't truly even embraced ourselves; we are not losing our relationships because many of them weren't real to begin with; we are simply losing the thing that we held onto for so long, the thing that has caused us pain without realising it, our facade, the mask that is truly attached to our face, and we believe it is us.

Many of us feel like we are right all the time; our opinion is right, our belief is right, and our actions are right. We hold onto the feeling of being right so much that we lock ourselves out of knowing the truth. How can you teach someone who thinks they know it all already?

We may have this feeling because we know what happens when we admit we were wrong. We were ridiculed many times for being wrong growing up. When we placed our hands up in class thinking we knew a question and found out that we were wrong, other students laughed and made fun, so in some cases we refused to put our hands up again. When we told our parents the truth, sometimes they would react badly, and so instead we grew up telling lies, holding onto those lies for dear life. When we made a mistake at our jobs, a lot of anger or frustration was projected our way; we were shouted at and punished, and so we became afraid of making mistakes. So here we are today, that person who went through those experiences, afraid to admit we were wrong because we knew the result of doing that; instead, we will admit we are right until we are blue in the face. Sometimes we do this for so long that eventually we do get proven wrong, and years of telling people we were right come flooding back. The anger people hold for us is there again—the very thing we tried to avoid. It's ironic, isn't it?

As I mentioned earlier, we feel that if we learned the truth, all the years we spent thinking otherwise were a waste of time. I do not look at it that way. The moment we realise the truth is a moment we have an opportunity to change; we might not have had that opportunity before, which is a problem when we do not question things right away.

You see, if we questioned things right away, we wouldn't have needed to change many years later; instead, an event occurred that forced us to realise the truth. Technically, it is a waste of time, but in a way, it is not, because if the moment we learned the truth, we changed, then we saved all the other years we could have spent if we hadn't learned it. We would have been in ignorance for even more time, so my advice to you, the reader, is not to think about it like you are wasting time; instead, think about how you are trying to save time. It is never too late to make a change and live with the effects of that change.

Bask in the ambience of your own desire for truth. Many people in the world who have religions, opinions, or beliefs do not see it this way, and so more time is bound to be wasted, never seeing the beautiful sunlight because they lay under the shade of their own "truth.".

The house theory is really my interpretation of the world around us. I feel it helps explain why we have so much trouble sometimes speaking the truth or hearing the truth, and as a result of that, we hold ourselves back from great possibilities. Yes, it is true. Even if my theory is correct, humankind has created and accomplished many great things. However, the problem is the negative emotions we carry and refuse to let go, whether we refuse to let them go because we do not believe we can let them go or we do not feel it is necessary. We will be forever bound to make the same mistakes, rarely having any desire to fix the actual cause, instead attempting to fix the effects as we chase after our own tail.

If we desire to see our facade, to see which 'houses' we belong to, remember this: If even the slightest bit of truth causes the smallest amount of resistance, we have already fooled ourselves as we hold up the foundations of a 'house' that is crumbling beneath our feet.

John Doe Diaries Part III

Who am I? A fellow member asked me the other day. I didn't know what to tell him, and I was also caught off guard by the question, as I had never felt the need to consider it. I tried to console him, tell him whatever name I could remember, and show him that it doesn't matter who he is because he has us. Suddenly, the thought struck me like lightning: who am I? I used to know my name, didn't I? It began with a K; I am sure of it. I would ask around to find out, but what would be the point, they'd only lie or question my loyalty like I did with the other one. It is strange; even though we are in this together, it feels as if we are alone to deal with our internal struggles.

As I am about to rest, the door swings open, and behind it is a bitter chill we have never felt before. We all hastily try and close the door, but the force is strong, but we are stronger. Eventually, we manage to get the door closed, but we are all exhausted, and as I look around at fellow members trying to catch a breath, I can hardly recognise any of them. Where has the time gone? The cold air still clings to the halls, and our past actions still echo throughout every room, haunting us. Is this it? The sacrifices we have made have all been for us to suffer in this place. I barely even know myself any more; I feel hollow. I often feel detached from myself as I watch myself repeat the same actions day in and day out. I wish things were as they used to be; it used to be warmer throughout these halls. Where did we go wrong?

The Solution

Hopefully, by this point, you can understand how important personal change is and why it is required, but in order to change something, we must first see things for how they truly are.

Since the beginning of the book, I have used the term 'we', when referencing certain actions we may have taken as humankind in history, and I did that because I still have some of the fears that I have mentioned and, in some way, I still contribute to the world's problems. I desire to remove my fear entirely so I can stop being part of the problem and become part of the solution. Even though sometimes I am still afraid to ask questions or sometimes I am still afraid to be my true self, my desire is there; I wouldn't have made the book if I didn't have the desire.

From this moment forward, in some areas, I am going to use the term "you." The reason is because I need you to realise how important you are as an individual and how much I believe in your ability to change. I don't want you to think I'm putting you in with everyone else when referring to how you can change as an individual because it is an individual process and no one else can do it for you. You have a unique personality that makes you special, and I desire for you to unleash that personality onto the world for all to see by openly questioning your own reality and beginning to see the truth and your truth as a result. Throughout this chapter, I will take you through the steps I believe are needed to become aware and begin to change the world around you in many loving ways. First up, humility...

Humility

Sometimes, I would often hear people say, "Oh, isn't this person humble?" when they were referencing when someone was really being modest and didn't want to take all the credit for doing something amazing. The Cambridge Dictionary defines humility as "the quality of not being proud because you are aware of your bad qualities." So we throw around the word humble quite often, but I have a different definition. To me, humility is a willingness to be in the moment and have a constant desire for personal truth, no matter what the circumstances. If we feel embarrassed, we admit it to ourselves and need to dig deeper to find out why; if we are afraid, we admit we are afraid and need to dig deeper to find out why. Humility, to me, is a constant search for truth in the moment and all the truth we could potentially know in the future. Now, sometimes searching for that truth will mean we will have to feel certain emotions we have never wanted to feel before. That is what humility is to me. It is almost like going back to having that childhood innate curiosity about everything and no longer locking ourselves down to what the world considers normal; we are beginning to strip away our facade and enter whole new possibilities.

Firstly, begin to question the actions of others inside the 'house'; you have been apart of the system for so long and may have turned a blind eye to the actions of others in the system out of fear. As part of society, we must collectively understand why we are so resistant to the truth to begin with and where exactly it went wrong. Build a desire to look through history and observe the emotions at the time. See what we are willing to do as a society to avoid hearing the truth and to avoid saying the truth. What are the results of our actions as a group? These are the things you must begin to question and realise.

While it can sometimes be depressing to see the results, you must remember that it doesn't have to stay that way and that if we allowed change to forever flow, we would not be in the situation we are in at the moment. As mentioned before in previous chapters, some of the most destructive organisations in the world have had horrendous results, but we have to see what our impact is on that from an emotional level and what the potential could be if we do not change today. Eventually, if you are open enough, you will come to the conclusion that something needs to change, and you are absolutely right; many things do have to change. You can equate it to slowly taking off the blindfold, inch by inch, and the world we helped to maintain is in ruin.

While being apart of the 'house' It is sometimes difficult to comprehend how people outside the 'house' feel and why they took certain actions against you. As part of the 'house' you may have believed in an eye for an eye and in believing that you helped them ignore their emotions as well by not acknowledging your own, and so of course they will react harshly to the actions you took; they will have the same lack of empathy that you have towards them. Acknowledge their emotions; see their sadness; see their anger; see their hatred; see it for what it was and how your actions caused them to have the same emotions; and vice versa.

Throughout the entirety of the slave trade in the United States of America, most white people of that generation did not care about the emotions of the people they made slaves; they did not care if they were sad or angry; they wanted what they wanted, and they wanted it now. Generations of people suffered as a result, and few white people in America today still have the same disposition that generations before them had. Of course, not many of us have done anything as bad as enslaving someone. I understand that. But that is the extreme it can lead too; we can become so desensitised to how other people feel we are okay with treating them in harsh ways; wake up from that; begin to see the results of the actions you and everyone in the 'house' once took and see that it is your individual responsibility to do something about it.

I would like to encourage you to figuratively look in the mirror and question in any given moment why you feel a certain way, and if we don't want to question it, begin to look at why we are afraid to. Sometimes the moment is not the right time to do it, so give yourself time when you are alone to be able to question it. We have to take time to pause and be willing to be open sometimes in the face of adversity. In that moment, you will likely feel a lot of resistance because you don't want to admit how you really feel. You may have been abused in many different ways. Imagine it like this for a moment..

You accidentally cut your finger, and instead of doing what you would typically do in that moment, you just let it fester over time. So every now and then, when you bump into it, your resistance to the pain causes you to lash out at whatever touched it. Even contemplating looking at the cut years later feels horrible because we would equate the level of pain to how it would look if we saw the reality of it. It is in that moment that we have a chance to realise that it is because of our decisions that we allowed it to get that bad, so you have to acknowledge how you feel in the moment by looking at it and going through the process of erasing the pain.

At this point, I would like to talk about developing your will. I believe some of you do not yet realise how much you have sacrificed your will and still sacrifice it on a daily basis. I personally am still learning about that, but I have made significant progress since the beginning.

Will is the actions we take at any moment. I'm not talking about willpower, which I believe is more of a form of forcing yourself to overcome something; I'm referring to the ability to willingly do something on your own without the use of force. Allow me to explain. Some of us might feel sad, so we might overeat, consume alcohol, or use some other substance; some may even rely on friends to pick us up. I feel these actions are a way of avoiding the emotion, really distracting us from the issue, and for many of us, these actions have become automatic; we do them without even thinking about it. You could say our will is stuck in a set of repeating actions, and developing that will to do something different takes time; it's like building a muscle. After repeating a more positive action, such as acknowledging the emotion and feeling it, it becomes easier over time, except this time, the outcome is much more positive. Using your will means that you are in control of your own actions, so it doesn't matter what we feel in any particular moment; we will not automatically take action in unloving ways like we have been doing; instead, we will desire to see what is causing this and then willingly seek out the truth.

We have become so reliant on people or things to help us avoid emotions. You must begin to go in the opposite direction and willingly look to not avoid things. I would often think about it like walking with a crowd of thousands or millions of people all going in one direction, and the moment we snap out of the direction we are going in because we realise where it is heading, developing your will is like choosing to face and walk in the other direction while everyone looks at you with disdain, questioning your decision. It is a conscious choice; no longer are you going to unconsciously follow the crowd. So developing your will to go the opposite way is just going to mean practising. The moment we feel fear, stay in the moment and do not react automatically. Desire is going to be a massive part of developing will, but I will talk about that later. Just remember, it's a process; be patient with it and have compassion for yourself.

Once you have admitted to yourself how you feel in the moment or later, when you have had a moment to yourself, you can now begin to look at how it has affected those around you because of your decision to ignore personal truth for so long. This part is quite difficult because the truth has been ignored for so long, and you begin to wake up from the dream and see how other people have felt about your actions.

For example, for not being aloud to be yourself, maybe when you were a child, you got angry or jealous at other people who were more themselves, or at least different from yourself. Another example from the opposite perspective is that you may have grown up thinking you were inferior to men, so you may have let them get away with things, and over time, by allowing yourself to be shut down, you may have developed resentment or hatred for them, which is something you might not have seen initially. The reality is that, as an individual, you are not inferior or superior and that you have something to offer the world that no one else can. You might not feel that right now, but through questioning and feeling it, I believe you will eventually learn that truth.

The last example I will give is this: you may have believed the right way to deal with a child is by spanking them, and because of that, you don't want to look at what effect that had on the child. You must have compassion for yourself because, at that moment, you could not see a better way. However, now you have the potential to see the truth of the matter and correct such actions.

In seeing all the effects you may have done to others and to yourself, you can finally realise one thing. You cannot expect anyone else to change first; we have done that for centuries, and it does not work. Not only does it not work, it is actually unfair, because by wanting them to change first, you are also condoning the problem. Begin to take responsibility by deciding you must act first if the world is to change.

Vision

Isn't your imagination beautiful? Well, at least I think it is. Having the vision to be able to see beyond the current reality and contemplate the possibilities is truly a remarkable and important ability. Although many of us have had dreams in the past that have not come true, I would implore you to stop living in the past and see your great potential.

We have begun to see, at least intellectually, some of the damage we have done to ourselves, others around us, and maybe even our environment, so what possibilities can you see? My all-time favourite quote is by Ghandi, which states, "Be the change you wish to see in the world." I have loved that quote from the moment I heard it. It's interesting how quotes, which are usually small sentences, can just spark something within us. But I loved the quote because it meant we have the responsibility to see the world change, no one else, and isn't that fantastic; if we had to rely on other people to change our reality, man, we would have serious problems. Although we, as a society, may have looked to the government to solve our deeper problems, our religion to solve our problems, or our significant other to solve our issues, I am telling you that I believe it is in your hands to solve all of the bigger problems in your life and assist in solving some of the problems in the world around you.

As a result of you taking responsibility, others will come along with you. Begin to imagine what effect you could have on the world and what it could mean for the world if you began to change. Also, begin to see the things you are interested in. No longer do your true desires have to be held back by your fears; allow your true self to stretch out and see which ways you can make positive changes in the world.

I once heard a story on YouTube channel called 'Business Insider' about an African woman named Ifedolapo Runsewe who had started a process to gather old tyres left in landfills and turn them into a brick shape that is softer and bouncier to be able to form floors for playgrounds. According to Business Insider, October 2023, *"Humans throw out around a billion tyres every year; recycling them gets expensive and complicated, so in most countries they just pile up in landfills. And here in Nigeria, they can help spread malaria."* Ifedolapo's idea to turn tyres into bricks for playgrounds was initially dismissed, and they actually thought she was crazy. As of the video, she has 100 full-time employees, and the business makes about 16 cents for every recycled tyre.

A truly brilliant story, although Ifedolapo only dents the existing problem, the reality is that it is a start and a brilliant one at that. I believe that all of us have the potential to take these kinds of actions. Of course, some of us are interested in other things, so we will have other goals, but having the vision to see what we want is a start. I cannot express to you how much I believe in that. Even after I have seen all the destructive things we as human beings have done, I believe we can change. The reason is this: it only takes one of us to spark that change, and in history, this has been a fact. If I inspire even one of you to visualise a different future and to go for it, I will be overjoyed.

Remember to think beyond what the world considers to be normal. The word 'normal' is just a way to limit yourself. If we are going to see a future where there is no more pain or suffering and the environment is in a much better state, we cannot live in the house of normality. Stretch the imagination as far as you can see, and even beyond that, I do believe nothing is out of reach.

I do not believe humans cannot live without fear; how could we possibly think that? I have already demonstrated how many of the world's problems eventually come down to fear, so at some point, in order to permanently change the world's current condition, fear can no longer be a factor. However, fear today is a normality, and even after you finish reading the book, the fear within you will still be a reality. But do not settle for the idea that it has to stay within you. If you are afraid of death, seek the truth about whether we actually die or not. You won't turn your nose up at hearing a medium; instead, you will question it constantly. If the medium cannot answer such questions, test if communication with people who have died is possible. Do not think of yourself as crazy. In my mind, it is crazy to hold onto a fear when we have no idea if it is true or not.

Do not stop questioning; do not stop being curious. It is the truth that will set you free. It is very difficult to sometimes have the vision to see past your pain or what it would be like to not have fear when we are currently living in fear. Believe me, I still struggle to see past it. As long as you stay in the moment, continuously questioning it, I believe you will begin to see the light at the end of the tunnel.

Desire

Desire is one of the most beautiful things I have ever come to understand, and I still don't understand it totally, but it is amazing. I love the fact that at any moment we can just have a desire to change something, and as a result of that, things do change. It is just remarkable. Seeing how one person can go from one end of the scale to the other. The Wright brothers desire to build a flying machine and Ifedolapo's desire to create playgrounds for children out of old rubber. It is truly astounding at the things human beings can change and how drastically we can change as well. Stanley 'Tookie' Williams was a great example of that change.

Williams was the founder of the gang in America known as the Crips, and I first saw his story in his biopic called 'Redemption: A Stan Tookie Williams Story', where Jamie Foxx played Stanley Williams.

When Williams was 6 years old, he and his mother moved to Los Angeles, California, in hopes of achieving a better way of life. Interestingly, Williams later recalled the look of the South Central neighbourhood he moved into: "a shiny apple rotting away at the core.".

Finding the street life more interesting than being at home, Williams began wondering around the neighbourhood, taking everything in, and as the new kid on the block, he had to quickly learn how to defend himself from the neighbourhood bullies as he would occasionally be thrown into physical conflicts. "As a member of the black male species living in the ghetto microcosm, circumstances dictated that I be either prey or predator." Williams later said this about his adolescence. "It didn't require deep reflection to determine which of the two I preferred." He would grow up to become immersed in a culture of violence and drugs, and without parental influence, Williams grew up idolising gang members and criminals who dealt drugs and did a number of other illegal acts. As the neighbourhood was violent, encouraged by gamblers and hustlers, betting progressed to fighting between young teens, and Williams was paid to box other young teenage boys into unconsciousness. It was experiences like this that hardened Williams, who kept the horrors he saw and performed from his mother.

Rather than regularly attend school, he believed he was better off in the streets and earning his reputation with his fists. Through fighting, he made several friends, and one of these friends was Raymond Washington, whom Williams met in 1969. The two boys formed an alliance that became known as the "Crips," a group they initially founded to protect the neighbourhood from larger gangs. The Crips consisted of 30 members, but they eventually divulged into the East-side and West-side Crips. By 1979, the Crips were a statewide gang, and Stanley Williams and Raymond Washington had lost control of the group. The division ultimately led to Williams and Washington's downfall; Washington was later shot and killed, and his murder was blamed on the Hoover faction of the Crips, which then led to war between Hoover and other Crip factions. In the same year, Williams was a major contributor to criminal acts; he and gang members had robbed a convenience store, and he apparently shot and killed the convenience store owner, although he would later deny killing the owner. He also broke into the office of the Brookhaven Motel and allegedly killed three members of the Taiwanese family who owned and operated the motel. A ballistics expert linked the shotgun shell at the motel to William's gun, and several gang members had testified that Williams had bragged about the crime. Williams also denied this shooting, claiming they were trying to set him up.

In 1981, Williams was tried and convicted in Los Angeles Superior Court of all four murders plus two counts of robbery, and he was sentenced to death. On April 20 of that year, he was sent to San Quentin State Prison to sit on death row. Williams did not adjust to prison life well, and by the mid-1980s, he had been given a six-and-a-half-year stay in solitary confinement for multiple assaults on guards and fellow inmates. After two years in solitary, Williams started to examine his life choices and repented for his past actions. This led him to begin speaking out against violence, and he thanked God for his transformation. He eventually filed for a federal appeal in 1988 and told court officials he was a changed man, but his appeal was denied. In 1994, he was released from solitary confinement. With the help of his new mindset, he began to write books, and in 1996, with the help of his co-author Barbara Cottman Becnel, he published the first of eight *Tookie Speaks Out Against Gang Violence* books aimed at children. The next year, he wrote an apology for his hand in creating the Crip Gang. "I am no longer part of the problem. Thanks to the almighty, I am no longer sleepwalking through life," he wrote.

At some point in 2002, Mario Fehr, a member of the Swiss Parliament, nominated Williams for the Nobel Peace Prize in recognition for his work against gang violence. Although he did not win the award, many of his supporters spoke out in favour of the former gang member's transformation. He would be nominated for the award six times in total. That same year, Williams appealed again for a commuted death sentence. The appeals panel desperately urged the judge to consider commuting William's death sentence, citing the former gang member's efforts towards anti-gang education. The appeal was once again denied. In 2004, Williams helped to create the Tookie Protocol for Peace, which was a peace agreement for one of the deadliest and most infamous gang wars in the country between the Crips and their rival, the Bloods. Williams continued to write an additional book, attempting to persuade kids to follow in his footsteps.

With his death coming closer and closer, Williams petitioned again for clemency in 2005. California Governor Arnold Schwarzenegger met with Williams to help decide whether the sentence should be commuted to life in prison. Williams' defenders had 30 minutes to plead their case to the governor. After the meeting, Schwarzenegger denied Williams bid for clemency, citing the forensic evidence linking him to the killings in 1979. Despite the apparent protests from the NAACP and various supporters who turned out to fight the decision, Williams was executed by lethal injection on December 13, 2005, at San Quentin State Prison.

A brilliant but sad story about a man seeing his former actions and the results and having a desire to not only change himself but to change any future possibility of children ending up committing the same actions he once did. I am a firm believer in giving someone an extra chance when they have shown true change, not just killing them because of the actions they took many years ago. We never know what a person is capable of until we give them that opportunity. It is our ability to change at the drop of a hat because of desire that gives us all such great potential.

Having a desire that is based around humility is what helps us to connect with who we truly are. If we are willing to seek the truth about everything, no matter what the initial desire looks like, it will end up being something amazing and beautiful. Having a true desire is action; it is the action of needing to change, which is amazing when you think about it. So even your desire right now to change something, even if it has not happened yet, is already an action; it is the first step to changing. It's an amazing feeling; it's like a fire is lit, and it warms us from head to toe because we know what the potential is; the true self is beginning to express itself.

A true desire craves truth like fire craves oxygen, so you begin to seek it in any form possible; you are no longer judging where you seek it either, and you would not judge others. You are willing to sit and listen to a lecture on the topic for hours, create notes, and expand on the idea in any way. You are also willing to do research by reading books or going on the internet and searching for answers. Through learning new truths from all the different ways you are getting closer and closer to achieving your goal, you are willing to experiment; failure no longer dampens your spirit; it charges it, ready for the next time you attempt the experiment. Unfortunately, many of us do allow failure to affect us including myself sometimes, but that is part of the process. Feel how disappointed you are, go deeper into that feeling, discover yourself, and you will become like an enthusiastic scientist, happily seeking the next truth to be unveiled.

This part of desire is arguably the most important and is still something I struggle with because of my fears. A true desire does not hide; it instead tells everyone who is willing to listen what you have discovered. If you think about it, when you were younger and you discovered something new, you would run up to your parents and show them or show your friends, and even if you don't remember, you still see kids doing this all the time. Learn to express yourself and be your true self all the time. It will not happen straight away; things do not change overnight, but it is the process that is the most beautiful part. It is knowing that within each step you have achieved something you did not achieve the day before, and as you look back at the view, you will have a greater perspective and understand where you came from and appreciation for where you are now.

Bravery

We often see bravery as standing up and fighting the people who may have done you or others wrong. This is not far from the truth, but it is not quite my interpretation of it. To me, bravery is going against the grain because you feel it is right, doing the opposite of what everyone else expects you to do; it is having the ability to acknowledge how we feel in the moment, no matter how much we are afraid of doing so. This is sometimes one of the most difficult actions we face in our lives. Harriet Tubman is a great example of bravery.

Harriet Tubman was born in 1820 on a plantation in Dorchester County, Maryland. Her mother was named Harriet Green, and her father was called Benjamin Ross. They originally named their daughter Araminta Ross and called her "Minty." Her mother worked as a cook in the plantation's "big house," and her father was a timber worker. Araminta later changed her first name to Harriet in honour of her mother. Harriet had eight brothers and sisters, but due to the realities of slavery, many of them were forced apart, despite Harriet's mother's attempt to keep them together. When Harriet was 5 years old, she was rented out as a nursemaid, where she was whipped when the baby cried, leaving her with permanent emotional and physical scars. Harriet was rented out for many different things, including setting muskrat traps and a field hand. She later said that she preferred physical plantation work to indoor domestic chores. Harriet's desire for justice became apparent at the young age of 12, when she spotted an overseer about to throw a heavy weight at a fugitive. Harriet stepped between the enslaved person and the overseer, and the weight struck her head. She later said this about this incident: "The weight broke my skull; they carried me to the house, all bleeding and fainting. I had no bed, no place to lie down on at all, and they laid me on the seat of the loom, and I stayed there all day and the next." The incident left Harriet with headaches and narcolepsy for the rest of her life, causing her to fall into deep sleep at random. Because of the damage caused by the weight, her infirmity made her unattractive to potential slave buyers and renters.

In 1840, Harriet's father was set free, and Harriet learned that her mother's will had her and her children, which included Harriet, set free. But her mother's new owner refused to recognise the will and kept the entire family in bondage. At some point in 1844, Harriet married John Tubman, a free black man, and additionally changed her last name from Ross to Tubman. The marriage was not good, and she gained knowledge that two of her brothers, named Ben and Henry, were about to be sold, which provoked Harriet to plan an escape. On September 17, 1849, Harriet, Ben, and Henry escaped their Maryland plantation. The brothers, however, changed their minds and went back. With the help of the Underground Railroad, Harriet persevered and travelled 90 miles north to Pennsylvania and freedom. Tubman went on to find work as a housekeeper in Philadelphia, but she wasn't satisfied living free on her own; she wanted freedom for her loved ones and friends too. Later on, she eventually returned south to lead her niece and her niece's children to Philadelphia via the Underground Railroad. At one point, she tried to bring her husband, John North, but he'd remarried and chose to stay in Maryland with his new wife.

In 1850, the Fugitive Slave Act allowed fugitive and freed workers in the North to be captured and enslaved. This evidently made Harriet's role as an Underground Railroad conductor even harder, and it forced her to lead enslaved people even further north to Canada, often travelling at night during the spring or fall when the days were shorter. Over the next 10 years, Harriet befriended other abolitionists such as Frederick Douglass, Thomas Garrett, and Martha Coffin Wright and eventually established her own Underground Railroad network. It is widely reported that she emancipated 300 enslaved people; however, those numbers may have been estimated and exaggerated by her biographer, Sarah Bradford, since Harriet herself claimed the numbers were much lower. Nevertheless, it is believed that Harriet personally led at least 70 enslaved people to freedom, including her elderly parents, and instructed dozens of others on how to escape on their own. She later claimed, "I never ran my train off track, and I never lost a passenger.".

When the Civil War broke out in 1861, Harriet found new ways to fight slavery. She was recruited to assist fugitive enslaved people at Fort Monroe and worked as a nurse, cook, and laundress. Harriet used her knowledge of herbal medicines to help treat sick soldiers and fugitive enslaved people. In 1863, Harriet became head of an espionage and scout network for the Union Army. She provided crucial intelligence to Union commanders about Confederate Army supply routes and troops, and she helped liberate enslaved people to form Black Union regiments. Though just over five feet tall, she was a force to be reckoned with, although it took over three decades for the government to recognise her military contributions and award her financially. In Harriet Tubman's later years after the Civil War, Harriet settled down with family and friends on land she owned in Auburn, New York. She married former enslaved man and Civil War veteran Nelson Davis in 1869 (her previous husband, John, died in 1867), and they adopted a little girl named Gertie a few years later.

In 1896, Harriet purchased land adjacent to her home and opened the Harriet Tubman Home for Aged and Indigent Coloured People. The head injury she had suffered in her youth was still causing her severe pain, and she underwent brain surgery to help relieve some of that pain. Her health, however, continued to deteriorate, eventually forcing her to move into her namesake rest home in 1911. Pneumonia took Harriet Tubman's life on March 10, 1913, but her legacy lives on.

Even against all the possible threats to her life, attempting to not only escape for herself but to then go back and help others escape is unfathomable. It is almost hard to even comprehend the kind of courage that took, which is truly tremendous. Although in the past it has only been very specific people who created great change in the world, I believe we all have the capability to do that, and what a world it would be if we did.

You have broken the illusion; you can now see things for what they are; you have the imagination to see beyond what your current condition is; and you have the desire to go there. It is time to stand tall and begin to take action. Do not falter; continue going full steam ahead because you know it is all on you; no one else will do it for you. Even in the case of the slaves who decided to escape thanks to Harriet Tubman's help, they still needed to move their own legs to reach freedom because no one else would move their legs for them. The old saying "you can take a horse to water, but you cannot force it to drink" comes to mind. The burden is on you, and yes, that burden will feel heavy, but the sweet nectar of your vision is hard to resist.

Embrace your mistakes bravely too. Do not be afraid to get something wrong; do not be afraid to believe in something you eventually find to be false. It is through mistakes that we can learn by seeing the result. Yes, the world around you will likely not forgive you for making those mistakes, but you know that if you do not keep moving and if you do not keep seeking the absolute truth, you will never accomplish your goal and forever repeat the same mistakes.

The neighbourhood is terrified. I say that because as you change, the people around you may become afraid that you will break their "reality," their dream, and as a result, they will not accept your desire and may attack. Understand the world's condition, see their unwillingness to break from the dream as a result of its condition, and understand that it is the people who were ready to die for what is right that made change for the rest of the world. They will not like it; they will not like the change you are indirectly forcing upon them. Through this time, it is only compassion and love for the neighbourhood that can help them see their reality, no matter how they treat you.

The last thing I want to say in this chapter is this: I believe in you, just like I have had to believe in myself. I believe in your ability to see forth a new world free of anguish; I believe in your ability to create a world far beyond our current capabilities of understanding; I believe in your ability to persevere and accomplish the things we never thought were possible; and I believe in your ability for our children to then never grow up in a world that we know of today.

My Final Message

My Experience

Growing up, I rarely considered change; rarely did I consider if I should change or even if I could. Most of the time I was clinging onto the present, and as the present moulded itself into tomorrow, it would force me to consider what my future would look like; sure, on occasions I did, but I never took it seriously. On many occasions, things would change around me; my friends moved house or became interested in other things, but there is one particular moment I remember that really brought me to the reality of the moment.

During my childhood, I would spend several weeks throughout the year at my cousins houses, both on my mother's and father's sides. I loved spending time there; both sets of cousins would teach me cool things I'd never forget and would appreciate as I got older. Most of them, baring one were older than I was, so as I grew older, they became interested in other things. At one point, spending the days I had off school at my cousins house, I found myself alone for the first time in a long time being there.

Most of the time, one of my cousins would want to hang out with me, but this time they were all gone, out experiencing the world.

Now, of course, I wasn't in the house alone; at that point, they had made sure that someone was in the house to look after me. It was at that moment that I felt like a hindrance, and I had to realise the reality of the situation. The reality was that all my cousins at that house, who were already 5 or more years older than me, were doing other things, like working, going clubbing, etc. From that moment, having realised the scope of the situation, I didn't go back there any more. I decided not to be a hindrance, but I had missed the point. In all my years of clinging to the present, it would eventually cause me to ignore my future. That was the lesson of that moment, but I missed it. For many years, still trying to cling onto the present and past, I would reminisce, thinking about the good times I had, once again ignoring my inevitable future.

The reason why I didn't like thinking about the future was primarily because I didn't want to take action; I wanted to sit on the fence and I wrongfully thought it would figure itself out. Anytime I tried to take actions regarding the future, I would eventually hit a wall. That wall was the feeling of really not wanting to do anything; it felt as if I was dragging myself, kicking and screaming, into the future. Now, anytime you have that kind of resistance, eventually the wall is going to become so big that I would just stop taking actions, stop doing the project I was doing, distract myself, and procrastinate. However, seeing what my inevitable future would look like if I decided not to take action, I would attempt actions and hit that wall over and over again. I was not getting the message or the results I desired. I desperately wanted to avoid that feeling; in fact, I wanted to avoid the feeling so much that I was willing to sacrifice my future as a result of it.

And yet...

I am writing this book and have put far more effort and time into this than any other project, and if you are reading it, then I must have finished it. The reality is that if I had started writing this book two years ago, which would have been in 2022, I would never have finished it; I would have hit the wall like I always did and would have given up as a result. Except this time there was a difference. Just over a year ago, I desired to feel the emotion I had been ignoring for decades. Once I hit that wall, I had to stop and allow myself to feel the emotion. Strangely, there was a lot of anger, and after allowing myself to feel the anger somewhat, behind it was sadness, and I allowed myself to feel that. Now the anger and sadness that I felt when encountering the wall are not completely gone, but they have been greatly reduced. So the wall has not seemed as big as it used to, and I no longer scorn my future; in fact, I cannot wait to see the things I hope to accomplish.

The change I have seen myself go through in the past year is incredible, but there is still much ahead of me. I find it interesting and love how, at the drop of a hat, we have the ability to change our direction. Boom, just like that, and we're off. Truly fascinating.

The House Theory. A group of individuals slowly losing their identity as they conform to what the house desires. Breaking from this house would be asinine for most; after all, who are we to tear down the house our ancestors built. The very walls and foundation were built out of their fear and are willingly maintained by our own.

John Doe Diaries Part IV

Can you feel it? The cold breeze that would cause any of us to shiver and clench our bodies for warmth, we must plaster over the holes in the walls, but... I swear, we've seen these holes before. We're all tired, and none of us know how we got here or how long it's been, but no, we cannot leave. If all else fails, we must huddle up for warmth, but there is little comfort in this house. In the darkest of nights and coldest of winters, I feel myself slipping away, breaking from the reality of this place, but it drags me back into reality with a sudden gust of wind. There it is again—the hole we just patched up. As light and cold air fill up the room once more, we must take action. Darkness takes over; just as we settle down, the door is forced wide open, but we cannot close it or barricade it this time. We have been forced to live in a small area within our own house, but this is better than nothing as we settle down once again in the cramped space we now have. I feel it. It's gentle this time, but I feel it none the less. Suddenly I realise, we never really had shelter; all we had was a box waiting to be blown away towards its inevitable destruction.

The John Doe Diaries do not represent even the average person's thought process whilst in the 'house', but what John Doe does represent is how we tend to act and how we are willing to remain in the 'house' at the expense of our own identity and happiness. It is only when we have been worn down, through decades of making the same mistakes, that we see reality for what it truly is. The 'house' is a prison we placed ourselves in so we didn't feel the bitter truth of the outside, an effective illusion. It was an illusion that made us think we needed to be protected from the outside when, in actuality, we were being devoured from within.

It doesn't matter whether you agree with me or not regarding any of the statements I have made. The world needs to change at a much faster rate than it has done before. We must begin to seek the truth about everything. Remember, we are born not knowing anything; it is okay not to know something. From the moment we open our eyes, we are curious; from the moment we attempt to walk, we are learning; but from the moment we enter that dark, soulless 'house', not only have we sold ourselves short, but we have lost all hope and begin to settle down for an eternity in darkness and decay. Do not let that be your end, my dearest brothers and sisters.

Yours truly

Arran James Mowatt

BIBLIOGRAPHY

Kendra Cherry, '10 of the Most Common Phobias', October 14, 2022, https://www.verywellmind.com/most-common-phobias-4136563, (*There are many different types of fears*), **Page 4**

Prince.com 'Prince Early Years', (Date Unconfirmed), https://becoming.prince.com/story/, (*prince*), **Page 10**

Sandra Kettler, 'Aileen Wuornos' December 19, 2023, https://www.biography.com/crime/aileen-wuornos (*serial killer streak*) **Page 17**

Rebecca Woodham, ' Montgomery Improvement Association', April 7, 2010, https://encyclopediaofalabama.org/article/montgomery-improvement-association-mia/, (*rosa parks*), **Page 19**

BlackPast, 'The Montgomery Bus Boycott', January 17, 2012, https://www.blackpast.org/african-american-history/1955-martin-luther-king-jr-montgomery-bus-boycott/, (*first speech as president*) **Page 19**

Laura Parker, 'The world's plastic pollution crisis, explained' February 21, 2004, https://www.nationalgeographic.com/environment/article/plastic-pollution, (*here are just a few facts about plastic pollution*) **Page 24**

National Park Service, 'Wright Brothers', (updated) August 22, 2017, https://www.nps.gov/articles/wright-brothers.htm, (*wright brothers*), Page 25

'World suffrage timeline', (updated) April 27, 2023, https://nzhistory.govt.nz/politics/womens-suffrage/world-suffrage-timeline, (Ministry for Culture and Heritage), (*women have suffered*) Page 28

Grahame Allen, Helena Carthew and Yago Zayed, 'Knife crime statistics England and Wales' October 13, 2023, https://commonslibrary.parliament.uk/research-briefings/sn04304/, (*knife crime*) Page 29

Nepal J Epidemiol, 'Exploring UK Knife crime an dits associated factors: A content analysis of online newspapers', December 12, 2022, https://www.ncbi.nlm.nih.gov/pmc/articles/PMC9886559/, (*lets take a look at street violence*), Page 29

Adeel Hassan, 'Emmett Till's Eduring Legacy', April 27, 2023, https://www.nytimes.com/article/who-was-emmett-till.html, (*turned a local murder*), Page 38

South African History Online, 'A history of Apartheid in South Africa', (date unconfirmed), https://www.sahistory.org.za/article/history-apartheid-south-africa, (*apartheid*), Page 41

NSPCC Learning, 'How many children experience sexual abuse?', February 2024, https://learning.nspcc.org.uk/research-resources/statistics-briefings/child-sexual-abuse/#:~:text=Child

%20sexual%20abuse%3A%20statistics
%20briefing&text=We%20don%27t%20know
%20exactly,UK%20have%20been%20sexually
%20abused.&text=Sexual%20abuse%20is%20usually
%20hidden%20from%20view, (*leading children's charity*), **Page 44**

History.com Editors, 'Crusades', June 7, 2010, https://www.history.com/topics/middle-ages/crusades, (*crusades*) **Page 46**

A & E Network, 'Leah Remini: Scientology and the Aftermath' December 19, 2016, (*scientology*) **Page 49**

Jackie Mansky, 'The True Story of the Death of Stalin', October 10, 2017, https://www.smithsonianmag.com/history/true-story-death-stalin-180965119/, (*death of stalin*) **Page 54**

Rosaleen Fenton, 'Lotto Curse – Brits whose lives were destroyed when they became millionaires', December 13, 2023, https://www.mirror.co.uk/news/uk-news/lotto-curse-brits-whose-lives-31663577, (*lottery*), **Page 57**

Zaw Thiha Tun, 'Theranos: A Fallen Unicorn', (updated) February 12, 2024, https://www.investopedia.com/articles/investing/0201 16/theranos-fallen-unicorn.asp#:~:text=2004%3A %20Theranos%20raised%20%246.9%20million,million %20in%20early-round%20funding, (*I will use the Theranos example*), **Page 60**

Monica Killen, 'Something To Declare: Australia's Cane Toad Problem', April 28, 2022, https://www.bluesci.co.uk/posts/something-to-declare-australias-cane-toad-problem, (*sugar cane industry*), Page 62

Biography.com Editors, 'Stanley Tookie Williams Biography', April 2, 2014, https://www.biography.com/crime-figure/stanley-tookie-williams, (*tookie*), Page 72

History.com Editors, 'Harriet Tubman' October 29, 2009, https://www.history.com/topics/black-history/harriet-tubman, (*tubman*), Page 75

Printed in Dunstable, United Kingdom